God Makes a Start

Genesis 1-11

Kevin Perrotta
Gerald Darring

**Six Weeks
with the Bible
for Catholic Teens**

6

Exploring
God's Word

LOYOLAPRESS.
CHICAGO

LOYOLAPRESS.

3441 N. ASHLAND AVENUE
CHICAGO, ILLINOIS 60657
(800) 621-1008
WWW.LOYOLABOOKS.ORG

Nihil Obstat	*Imprimatur*
Reverend Michael Mulhall, O. Carm.	Most Reverend Edwin M. Conway, D.D.
Censor Deputatus	Vicar General
January 9, 2004	Archdiocese of Chicago
	January 10, 2004

The *Nihil Obstat* and *Imprimatur* are official declarations that a book is free of doctrinal and moral error. No implication is contained therein that those who have granted the *Nihil Obstat* and *Imprimatur* agree with the content, opinions, or statements expressed.

New Revised Standard Version Bible, copyright 1989, Division of Christian Education of the National Council of the Churches of Christ in the United States of America. Used by permission. All rights reserved.

23 From an interview with Dom Helder Camara, which appeared originally in "Voice in the Wilderness," by Oriana Fallaci, *The Sign,* July/August 1976.

34 From the Latin text ot St. Augustine's commentary *De Genesi ad Litteram libri XII,* which can be found in J.-P. Migne, ed., *Patrologia Latina* (Paris, 1887), vols. 34–35, cols. 245–486. Translation by the author.

36–37 Based on the Syrian text of St. Ephrem the Syrian's *Hymns of Paradise,* which can be found in Edmund Beck, ed., *Des Heiligen Ephraem des Syrers Hymnen de Paradiso,* Corpus Scriptorum Christianorum Orientalium, vol. 174 (Louvain: Secretariat du Corpus SCO, 1957). Translation by the author.

46 From the Greek text of St. John Chrysostom's homily on Genesis 17, which can be found in J.-P. Migne, ed., *Patrologia Graeca* (Paris, 1862), vol. 53, cols. 134–48. Translation by the author.

58–59 From Jacques Fesch's reflections in Augustin-Michel Lemonnier, ed., *Light over the Scaffold and Cell 18: The Prison Letters of Jacques Fesch* (New York: Alba House, 1996).

70–71 Jean Vanier's reminiscences are from his book *An Ark for the Poor* (New York: Crossroad Publishing, 1995).

70 The prayer by Jacqueline d'Halluin can be found in Kathryn Spink, *Jean Vanier and l' Arche: A Communion of Love* (New York: Crossroad Publishing, 1991).

82 From Joseph Miya, "Why I Like Being a Missionary Kid" at http://laymissioners.maryknoll.org/index.php.

Cover and Interior Design: Th!nk Design Group

ISBN 0-8294-2050-9

Printed in the United States of America.
04 05 06 07 08 Bang 5 4 3 2 1

Contents

How to Use This Guide

You might compare this booklet to a short visit to a national park. The park is so large that you could spend months, even years, getting to know it. But a brief visit, if carefully planned, can be worthwhile. In a few hours you can drive through the park and pull over at a handful of sites. At each stop you can get out of the car, take a short trail through the woods, listen to the wind blowing in the trees, and get a feel for the place.

In this booklet we'll drive through the first 11 chapters of Genesis, which contain the Bible's accounts of creation and the beginning of the human race. We will be able to take a leisurely walk through each account, thinking carefully about what we are reading and what it means for our lives today. While these chapters of Genesis are only a small fraction of the entire Bible, they touch on central themes in God's revelation to us: God's creative purposes for us, the effects of sin on our relationship with God, and God's continuing faithfulness toward us.

This guide provides everything you need to explore Genesis 1 through 11 in six discussions, or to do a six-part exploration on your own. The introduction on page 6 will prepare you to get the most out of your reading. The weekly sections provide explanations that highlight what the words of Scripture mean for us today. Equally important, each section supplies questions that will launch you into fruitful discussion, helping you to explore Genesis for yourself and to learn from one another. If you're using the booklet by yourself, the questions will spur your personal reflection.

Each discussion is meant to be a *guided discovery*.

Guided ~ None of us is equipped to read the Bible without help. We read the Bible *for* ourselves but not *by* ourselves. Scripture was written to be understood and applied in and with the church. So each week "A Guide to the Reading," drawing on the work of both modern biblical scholars and Christian writers of the past, supplies background and explanations. The guide will help you grasp the message of Genesis. Think of it as a friendly park ranger who points out noteworthy details and explains what you're looking at so you can appreciate things for yourself.

Discovery ~ The purpose is for *you* to interact with God's Word. "Questions for a Closer Look" is a tool to help you dig into the Genesis accounts and examine them carefully. "Questions for Application" will help you discern what these stories mean for your life here and now. Each week concludes with an "Approach to Prayer" section that helps you respond to God's Word. The supplementary "Living Tradition" and "Saints in the Making" sections offer the thoughts and experiences of Christians past and present in order to show you what Scripture has meant to others—so that you can consider what it might mean for you.

If you are using this booklet for individual study, pay special attention to the questions provided for each week (Warm-Up Questions, Questions for a Closer Look, Questions for Application). One advantage of individual study is that you can take all the time you need to consider all the questions. I also suggest that you read the first 11 chapters of Genesis in their entirety, and you will find that the "Between Discussions" pages will help you understand the portions of Genesis not covered in this booklet. Take your time making your way through Genesis 1–11 and this accompanying guide: let your reading be an opportunity for these stories to become God's words to you.

Exploring Our Beginnings

We're all fascinated by beginnings—the beginning of a new school year, the beginning of a new sports season. One beginning that particularly intrigues us is the big bang, that first moment when a mysterious little gift package of particles and forces arrived from nowhere, unwrapped itself, and exploded into a universe of galaxies, planets, mountain ranges, oak trees, and robins. The beginning of the universe attracts us because it is *our* beginning.

So it is natural for us to be intrigued by Genesis. Genesis is the book famous for the opening words, "In the beginning . . ." The first 11 chapters recount the origins of the universe and humankind. These are God-inspired accounts of our beginnings. Of course we are interested.

When we open the Bible to the first page, however, things seem strange by modern standards. Genesis is unlike modern books on cosmic or human origins. It doesn't give us an astronomer's account of a big bang and an expanding universe, nor does it give us a biologist's sketch of life evolving over a billion years. In Genesis 1 the interval from dark emptiness to human beings is spanned in six days. We won't find a paleontologist's report on early toolmaking hominids, but vivid, tragic tales of creation, harmony, sin, and judgment.

Most of us are very familiar with the stories of Genesis. Pretty much everyone has heard of Adam and Eve, Cain, and Noah. It's hard for us to appreciate how unusual these stories are. Nevertheless, it should not take you too long to realize that the types of writing we meet in Genesis chapters 1–11 are also different from those we are familiar with today.

The main reason for this difference is that the authors of Genesis belonged to a world quite unlike our own. They lived before the rise of scientific thinking. They did not have modern methods of writing history. They expressed their thoughts through stories. This is not to say they were primitive or unintelligent. They were as capable of wisdom as any later people, and they had God's guidance in composing the work that he intended. Nevertheless, the book they produced is the product of *their* culture, not ours.

As a result, the Genesis accounts do not fit neatly into our categories of thought. To help you understand this point, picture yourself as the librarian in charge of your school's library. Someone donates to the library the first 11 chapters of Genesis, which have been published as a separate book. When the slender volume arrives, you have to decide where to shelve it. First you survey the nonfiction side of the library. Should it go with works on astronomy? biology? history? You examine the book closely and decide it doesn't belong in any of those categories. You can't put it in the psychology section either, despite its interesting descriptions of dysfunctional families. So you turn to the fiction side of the library. What about shelving the book with collections of short stories? But you quickly realize that the Genesis accounts are documents of religious instruction, not imaginative works of art. Feeling somewhat frustrated, you consider shelving the book with collections of mythology. Yet the Genesis accounts are different from myths in important respects.

You would be puzzled about what kind of book Genesis is because the authors of Genesis combined elements that modern authors keep distinct. People in the ancient Near East would have been familiar with the combination of ingredients in Genesis. But for us modern people, Genesis is virtually unique.

It might help you to read many of the Genesis accounts as if you were reading a parable. A parable is an imaginative story that communicates a truth and spurs us to think. Jesus delivered much of his teaching through parables. The account of Adam and Eve, for example, is not a historical narrative but a parable-like story that brings out certain meanings. But keep in mind that the Genesis stories are only similar to parables; they aren't actually parables. Parables are pure fiction, but some actual events lie behind the Genesis accounts. Those events are not conveyed in straightforward scientific or historical language, but they are not fictional.

If people a couple of centuries ago had appreciated the parable-like nature of the Genesis accounts, we might not today be caught up in a lot of unnecessary arguments between advocates of science and advocates of the Bible. Many Christians think they are defending the Bible against theories that contradict it when they refuse to accept evolution as an explanation of the development of species, especially human beings. They do not realize that the authors of the Genesis stories do not intend to convey scientific or historical information. Their stories, therefore, cannot be in contradiction of scientific or historical findings. The narrator of Genesis, for example, was not concerned with *how* God brought humans into existence, and in fact he offered different descriptions of the process. Chapter 1 states that God "created" us (1:27), using a Hebrew word that never means making one thing from another. Yet chapter 2 says that God "formed" a man from dust and "made" a woman from the man's rib (2:7,22). Evidently the narrator was telling his readers *that* God created humans, not *how* God did it.

So we do not have to defend the Genesis account of human creation against the proponents of evolution. We can leave it to biologists to speculate about the processes by which humans developed. No biological discoveries can disprove the Genesis message that God created the human race, since in creating us God could have chosen any process that biologists might ever discover.

Parables are very brief, usually making only a single point or two. Because of their simplicity, parables raise questions for which there are no answers. Keeping this limitation in mind will save us from asking the wrong questions as we read Genesis. For example, we may wonder what kind of legs the snake had before God cursed it (3:14) or where Cain's wife came from (4:17) or how Noah and his family could possibly have taken care of so many animals on the ark (7:1–24). These questions are unanswerable because parables are just not designed to answer questions like that.

Recognizing the parable-like quality of the Genesis accounts keeps us from getting hung up in pointless arguments and unanswerable questions. This frees us to focus on the meaning of the accounts. The authors of Genesis wrote to shed light on basic questions about human existence. It may be helpful to identify some of those questions before we begin our reading.

Chapter 1 in Genesis deals particularly with "what" questions:

➤ What is the universe? Most ancient Near Eastern people thought that the universe was made up of three orders of beings: gods who are a part of nature, nature that is filled with gods, and human beings, who are dependent on both. Genesis 1 is different: it elevates God far above nature and strips nature of any divinity.

➤ What is the place of humans in the scheme of things? Ancient people thought that humans were slaves of the gods, or maybe playthings of divine forces, or perhaps intelligent work animals. The way they saw it, humans were at the mercy of countless gods and demons and had to struggle to stay on the good side of those gods and demons. Genesis 1 gives a radically different answer to the question.

In chapters 2 and 3, questions of meaning and purpose predominate. For example:

➤ Why is the drive for union between man and woman so strong? What is the meaning of this mystery?

➤ What is the natural status of woman in relation to man?

➤ Why are relationships between men and women often marked by shame and exploitation?

➤ Why do human beings, who feel so at home in the world, meet such resistance from the natural environment? Why is getting food so hard? Why are animals strangers, even enemies?

➤ Why does the great blessing of childbearing involve such pain?

- Why do we have to die?

- Why don't snakes have legs? (Not all questions in Genesis are deep, theological ones.)

Key questions in later chapters include the following:

- In light of the barbaric ways in which humans sometimes treat each other, why doesn't God bring the human race to an end?

- Why do people, who have such intelligence, often fail to understand each other?

Obviously, these questions concern us too. While Genesis was written in a culture different from ours, it deals with universal human issues. We can grasp the point of Jesus' parables about the Kingdom of God, even without knowing a lot about the Galilean fishing and farming to which he referred. Just so, with a little study, we can grasp the basic messages of the Genesis stories without being experts on the ancient Near East.

The Genesis accounts deal with God's creation of the whole universe, but they focus on his relationship with his human creatures. They present us with very different pictures of God and humans. God emerges as a lover of good, a patient judge, a fatherly figure who wants what is best for his human children and is willing to make a new start with them when they mess up. Humans, on the other hand, show themselves to be a mixture of nobility and vice. They are intelligent and creative, capable of doing right, but inclined to transgress their creaturely limits and fatally attracted to the false notion that they can do without God.

It took many centuries for the early chapters of Genesis to be developed, and for many more centuries they have been read, studied, and interpreted in Israel and in the Church. Reading these accounts at the beginning of the 21st century, we are heirs of a tradition of writing and interpretation that stretches back more than 3,000 years. If we want to understand the accounts and see how they apply to us, we should know something about this tradition.

Scholars have studied the writings of other peoples in the ancient Near East, and they have learned that the origins of many Genesis stories go far back, to a period before Israel existed. In other words, both the Israelites and their neighbors who did not believe in the God of Israel inherited many of the same mythic descriptions of the beginning of the world from older Near Eastern culture.

Over centuries, as the people of Israel interacted with God, they came to a view of reality different than their neighbors. Consequently they reshaped the inherited stories to reflect their own very different picture of God, the world, and human beings. The result was stories that were still similar to those of their neighbors but that now carried new, divinely inspired messages.

The flood story is an example of this process. The Israelites and the Akkadians (who were from present-day Iraq) both drew on very ancient traditions of a catastrophic flood. In the Akkadian version of the story, the gods bring the flood because people were bothering them with noise. The Israelites, however, had discovered that God is not bad-tempered but just, and they reflected this knowledge in their version of the story. In the biblical telling, God brings the flood because he is saddened by people's violent oppression of each other. The Israelite story portrays a God who is righteous and compassionate, rather than capricious and self-concerned. Thus at one stage the accounts of the beginning served to sketch a truer portrait of God than that held by Israel's neighbors.

The accounts acquired another level of meaning when they were incorporated in the growing book of Scripture. Contrary to what we might expect, the accounts of the beginning were not the first part of Genesis to be included in the Bible. The narratives of God's dealings with Abraham and his family and of the exodus from Egypt were composed earlier. Later the accounts of the beginning were placed in front. By combining them with the history of God's dealings with Israel, the message came across that the God who had been unfolding a merciful plan for the people of Israel was not just the tribal God of Israel; he was the God of the whole universe. Thus the Genesis stories implied that God's activity on behalf of Israel must be part of a larger plan for the entire human race.

The Genesis stories reached a third stage of meaning with the coming of Jesus. God achieves his original purposes for the universe through his Son, who has now taken on human nature in Jesus of Nazareth. Since God's creative purposes find their fulfillment in Jesus, the creation accounts in Genesis reveal their deepest meaning when viewed in relation to him. Now that God's Son has come in human flesh, the Genesis accounts help us understand who Jesus is and what he has come to do.

The stories of Adam and Eve, of their sons Cain and Abel, of the people who provoked the flood and those who built the tower of Babel: all of these stories display our human tendency to overstep our limits as creatures, to take control of our lives apart from God, to treat one another unjustly. The Genesis accounts tell us that our unhappiness stems from our failure to trust and obey our creator. Against this background, Jesus' life and death emerge as a deliberate reversal of the deep-rooted human tendency to distrust and disobey God. Saint Augustine writes that Jesus "did not come to do his own will but the will of God by whom he was sent. In this he differed from Adam who chose to do his own will, not the will of his creator." Jesus' death and resurrection become understandable as the divine means of putting an end to our rebellion—symbolized in the Genesis accounts—in order to give us a fresh start in relationship with God (Romans 6:3–10). Just as Adam was the first human being, through whom we have received our human life flawed by sin, so Jesus is the new Adam, through whom we receive a life cleansed of sin and enlightened by the presence of God's Spirit (Romans 5:12–19; 1 Corinthians 15:21–22,45).

The early Church saw a clear connection between God's initial purposes revealed in Genesis and the fulfillment of those purposes through Jesus. It is not surprising, then, that the early Church used the Genesis accounts to help explain Jesus. For example, it viewed the cross on which Jesus died as a "tree" corresponding to the tree in the garden of Eden. At the first tree the human race lost its original relationship with God by distrust and disobedience; it regained this relationship with God through Jesus' trust and obedience at the second tree.

As centuries have passed in the life of the Church, Christians asking questions about God's plan have returned again and again to the Genesis accounts of beginnings. Saint Augustine, who died in the early fifth century, investigated Genesis as he tried to understand how there came to be any evil in a universe created by a perfectly good and powerful God. Augustine and later theologians have looked to Genesis for help in understanding the destabilizing effects of Adam's and Eve's disobedience (what theologians refer to as original sin) and how these effects are passed from one generation to another. In the late 20th century, Pope John Paul II intensively explored the account of Adam and Eve to shed light on the relationship between the sexes and on the "nuptial meaning of the body." The author of Genesis did not directly address these subjects, yet Genesis will always be part of Christians' efforts to deal with such issues.

Scripture is the soul of theology, the bishops of Vatican II pointed out. It is meant to be the soul of our own reflections. Just as the greatest Christian thinkers have repeatedly pondered the opening chapters of Genesis, so may we also read and reread them, seeking to understand God's relationship with us and his purpose for our lives. As we read, the Spirit who guided the narrator of Genesis to write will be with us, guiding us to understand and to act, to wonder and to praise.

Let There Be Light!

Warm-Up Questions

1 For you, this last week has been
- ○ ordinary
- ○ unusual
- ○ boring
- ○ great
- ○ a time of grace
- ○ a week to forget

2 Describe a memorable beginning in your life. How did it turn out?

3 If you could make a fresh start in some area of life, what would you change?

Opening the Bible

Genesis 1:1–31

The Universe: Act One, Scene One

1:1 In the beginning when God created the heavens and the earth, 2 the earth was a formless void and darkness covered the face of the deep, while a wind from God swept over the face of the waters. 3 Then God said, "Let there be light"; and there was light. 4 And God saw that the light was good; and God separated the light from the darkness. 5 God called the light Day, and the darkness he called Night. And there was evening and there was morning, the first day.

6 And God said, "Let there be a dome in the midst of the waters, and let it separate the waters from the waters." 7 So God made the dome and separated the waters that were under the dome from the waters that were above the dome. And it was so. 8 God called the dome Sky. And there was evening and there was morning, the second day.

9 And God said, "Let the waters under the sky be gathered together into one place, and let the dry land appear." And it was so. 10 God called the dry land Earth, and the waters that were gathered together he called Seas. And God saw that it was good. 11 Then God said, "Let the earth put forth vegetation: plants yielding seed, and fruit trees of every kind on earth that bear fruit with the seed in it." And it was so. 12 The earth brought forth vegetation: plants yielding seed of every kind, and trees of every kind bearing fruit with the seed in it. And God saw that it was good. 13 And there was evening and there was morning, the third day.

Creatures of Sea, Air, and Land

14 And God said, "Let there be lights in the dome of the sky to separate the day from the night; and let them be for signs and for seasons and for days and years, 15 and let them be lights in the dome of the sky to give light upon the earth." And it was so. 16 God made the two great lights—the greater light to rule the day and the lesser light to rule the night—and the stars. 17 God set them in the dome of the sky to give light upon the earth, 18 to rule over the day and over the night, and to separate the light from the

darkness. And God saw that it was good. [19] And there was evening and there was morning, the fourth day.

[20] And God said, "Let the waters bring forth swarms of living creatures, and let birds fly above the earth across the dome of the sky." [21] So God created the great sea monsters and every living creature that moves, of every kind, with which the waters swarm, and every winged bird of every kind. And God saw that it was good. [22] God blessed them, saying, "Be fruitful and multiply and fill the waters in the seas, and let birds multiply on the earth." [23] And there was evening and there was morning, the fifth day.

[24] And God said, "Let the earth bring forth living creatures of every kind: cattle and creeping things and wild animals of the earth of every kind." And it was so. [25] God made the wild animals of the earth of every kind, and the cattle of every kind, and everything that creeps upon the ground of every kind. And God saw that it was good.

God's Masterpiece

[26] Then God said, "Let us make humankind in our image, according to our likeness; and let them have dominion over the fish of the sea, and over the birds of the air, and over the cattle, and over all the wild animals of the earth, and over every creeping thing that creeps upon the earth."

[27] So God created humankind in his image,
    in the image of God he created them;
    male and female he created them.

[28] God blessed them, and God said to them, "Be fruitful and multiply, and fill the earth and subdue it; and have dominion over the fish of the sea and over the birds of the air and over every living thing that moves upon the earth." [29] God said, "See, I have given you every plant yielding seed that is upon the face of all the earth, and every tree with seed in its fruit; you shall have them for food. [30] And to every beast of the earth, and to every bird of the air, and to everything that creeps on the earth, everything that has the breath of life, I have given every green plant for food." And it was so. [31] God saw everything that he had made, and indeed, it was very good. And there was evening and there was morning, the sixth day.

Questions for a Closer Look

1 How does God's evaluation of his work in verse 31 differ from his previous evaluations? What might be the significance of this difference?

2 What are animals and humans allowed to eat? What, then, shouldn't they eat, and why shouldn't they eat it?

3 If this story were our only source of information about God, what would our picture of God be like?

4 Most ancient Near Eastern people thought of the sun, moon, and stars as gods. What would verses 14–18 say about such a belief?

A Guide to the Reading

Picture a movie scene that includes the use of cartoon-type animation. An artist sitting at an easel begins to paint. She sweeps her brush in broad strokes back and forth across the canvas. Through animation, at each stroke objects magically appear. With one stroke of the brush, a tree springs into view. Another stroke and a meadow surrounds the tree. Two dabs of the brush put a sun in the sky and a child beneath the tree. Suddenly the picture comes to life. The tree's branches sway in the breeze. The child runs across the meadow.

Genesis 1 is like that. God calls forth the universe in six days, each day an effortless stroke of an artist's brush. The account does not describe the processes by which the universe took shape and life developed, just as the animation does not show how an artist actually paints a picture. But Genesis teaches us things we cannot learn from astronomy or biology.

When you tell a story, you must say when and where the action begins. The problem in Genesis is that before creation there *was* no time or place. Nothing had been created, so the narrator describes the "situation" before creation: a shapeless emptiness, a watery darkness whipped by storms (the "wind from God" in verse 2 is probably a Hebrew way of describing an extremely violent wind). The narrator describes what cannot really be described, because it did not exist. (Keep in mind that, although I talk about "the narrator" or "the author" in this booklet, Genesis probably had several authors and editors.)

The author does not describe creation from nothing in quite the way that we have come to understand it. At the same time, he does not say that anything existed before God created. So when we see God performing operations on the watery darkness (1:6–10), this does not mean that God formed the world out of matter that already existed, for the dark ocean of verse 2 is not neutral matter in our modern sense. It is chaos, sinister nothingness, absence of any possibility of life. The account of God's bringing light to darkness and dividing waters (1:3–10) is a way of saying that God called into existence an orderly universe.

It seems strange that God creates light on the first day, while sun and stars appear only on the fourth, but the narrator is pursuing a logic of his own. The purpose of the light is to inaugurate time, and that is why God names Day and Night (1:5). Next God creates space. He establishes vertical space by engineering the sky, which ancient people thought of as a hard, transparent dome holding up a vast, blue ocean (1:6–8). God makes horizontal space by clearing away water to expose the land (1:9–10).

God called earth "Earth" and seas "Seas" (1:10) because in the culture of the time, name-giving indicated possession (see Isaiah 43:1). Thus the account shows that the universe is God's property; it belongs to him. Notice that God does not name the animals (keep this in mind for next week).

After creating various creatures (1:20–25), God reaches the climax of his efforts. Here he does not merely utter a "Let there be." God deliberates with himself—"Let us make" (1:26)—carefully considering his greatest undertaking.

God creates humans in his "image" and "likeness" (1:26–27). In the ancient Near East, kings were considered images of the gods. Thus for humans to be made in the image of God means that each of us has a "royal" dignity. God has made each of us with the intelligence and freedom required to carry out a royal assignment. God assigns us as his viceroys to govern the earth and its creatures (1:26).

Being made in God's image means even more than this, for it also means that we *correspond* to God. We are made like God in order to interact with him. There is a fit, a match, between God and us that makes a relationship possible. Indeed, our entire physical and spiritual nature is set up for a relationship with God. As soon as the first human couple stands before him, God activates this relationship. We read for the first time, "God said to them" (1:28). Human beings are the only creatures with whom God can carry on a conversation.

Questions for Application

1 How can it affect a student when there is turmoil at school? at home? among his or her friends? How can the turmoil in other parts of the world affect a young person's life?

2 Genesis tells us that the universe belongs to God: what difference should that make in how we treat the earth? God has put in your hands a tiny part of creation—your clothes, your CD player, your school supplies, your pet. If you were to consider these things as God's personal possessions, how might you relate to them differently?

3 What might this week's reading say about the belief that the movements of the stars and planets determine the course of people's lives?

4 How do you think God communicates to us that he is seeking a more personal relationship with us? What can we do to respond more fully to his invitation?

5 God gives the whole human race the mandate to "be fruitful and multiply, and fill the earth" (1:28). It is the mandate parents follow in giving birth to their children. If you have children one day, what would you want them to be like?

Approach to Prayer

Now that you have read the repeated divine declarations that "it is good," it is your turn to reflect them back to God in a litany of thanks:

First recite Genesis 1:31 with the group: "God saw everything that he had made, and indeed, it was very good."

Listen as others in the group mention things for which they are grateful, pausing after each item to pray together, "Thank you, Lord, for the goodness of your creation."

Recite Genesis 1:31 one more time with the group. Close by praying Psalm 8.

Saints in the Making

God and Our Chaos

In Genesis 1 creation is an ordering of chaos. God shatters the darkness of nonexistence by creating light, then joins darkness as a subordinate to the light in the alternating rhythm of night and day (1:1–5). God rolls back the lifeless deep; the tamed waters are assigned now to a place beside the land and become the bright sea (1:6–10).

God imposes order on chaos, but tendencies to fall apart and lose meaning remain. In the Israelite view, night and ocean continue as zones of danger. They are symbols of the destruction that lurks at the edges of life. Creation constantly needs the Creator to keep bringing the dawn, to keep holding back the floodwaters from the dry land.

Many young people experience chaos in their lives. They are confused about the direction in which their lives are going and are not even sure if they know in what direction they ought to go. They miss the things of childhood but are glad they have grown beyond childhood. They long for adulthood but are fearful of the obligations it will bring. They feel that no one understands the tensions in their lives, and yet they want very much to talk with someone who might understand.

Sometimes there is chaos in the lives of young people because of the actions of others. Parents argue and fight, they may even separate and divorce, and their children's lives are thrown into turmoil. One friend may turn against another and spread rumors that have no basis in truth. A thoughtless teacher may humiliate a student in front of the class, or an unreasonable administrator may treat a student unjustly.

At other times, the chaos is self-imposed as the young person looks for peace and satisfaction in all the wrong places. Experimentation with drugs, sexual encounters, excessive risk-taking, and fast living—these things can turn a young life inside-out.

Of course, there can be chaos at any stage in life. The late Dom Helder Camara, archbishop of Recife, Brazil and human rights advocate, spoke of getting up in the morning and having to "gather up the pieces I've scattered during the day—an arm here, a leg there, the head who knows where. I sew myself back together again." Throughout our lives we need the Genesis image of a chaos-ordering God standing before us as a sign of hope.

Between Discussions

L et's suppose that you are visiting relatives in another state and you have met someone your own age. Your new friend asks about your school, and you tell him or her about the yearbook and the French club. Your new friend would not notice anything, but if some of your classmates were standing next to you and heard what you said, they might wonder why you did not also mention the football team or the drama club. The fact is that we all tend to leave things out in our description of persons, places, and experiences.

We modern readers may not immediately notice, but the narrator of Genesis has also left out some features that his non-Israelite neighbors would have expected in a creation account. Most notably he has left out of his account any mention of other gods.

Many ancient Near Eastern people imagined that the world came into existence as the result of a battle between gods. They tended to think of creation as a laborious process in which gods made some things from other things. Genesis 1 has none of this. God creates without struggling with other gods because, quite simply, there aren't any. He commands, and things come into existence.

In one ancient creation myth, a certain god slays another god, called Sea, who has the form of a sea monster, and uses the corpse to construct the world. The author of Genesis knew this story and rejected it. In Genesis the sea is not divine; the "deep" in 1:2 is simply an image of chaos, of nonbeing. The sea does not emerge until the third day (1:9–10) and is merely an element of creation. Sea monsters are just the biggest, oddest pets in God's global aquarium (1:21).

Ancient readers would have been struck especially by the Genesis narrator's treatment of the sun, moon, and other heavenly bodies (1:14–18). Near Eastern people saw these things as gods who ruled human lives. Genesis 1 firmly demotes them from divine status. First, God creates all heavenly bodies. Second, they do not appear until the fourth day. They have no light of their own but merely transmit light already created (1:3). They serve to mark the passage of time and the occurrence of holidays (1:14); that is all. Far from being gods, they are nonentities: they do not even have names (see 1:16).

The narrator of Genesis was writing at a time when people thought that the universe was crowded with warring gods. He offered a simpler, yet deeper, view: one God has created everything. This God is not a power *within* the universe—a power of sun or sea or storm or sex. He is *the* power that has brought every other power into existence. Therefore we humans should worship, revere, listen to, and love this God alone. There is no need to worry about placating any other gods.

In many places in the world, this is a very relevant, up-to-date, and countercultural message. Think of India, for example. But what about us living in Western societies? Our public spaces and institutions are secularized. We do not meet statues of gods in schools or supermarkets or courtrooms. In our society, people look for scientific, rather than mythic, explanations of the origin of things. On the other hand, many people in our society believe that human lives may be influenced by stars, by magic, by supernatural beings of various kinds, by spiritual forces working through places or crystals, by the minds of the dead channeled through human teachers.

Genesis 1, then, carries a twofold message for us. First, in the face of growing beliefs in a variety of spiritual powers, Genesis declares absolutely that God is the only deity in the universe. From top to bottom, the universe is God's creation, inhabited only with the creatures that God has put there. Second, as we conduct our lives in secularized settings—in school, in sports, in entertainment—Genesis reminds us that no time or place exists apart from God. The universe is not meaningless matter; time is not an emptiness filled only with human sound and fury. All places and times, and we ourselves, are the handiwork and possession of a personal God.

The First Marriage

Warm-Up Questions

1 What is the nicest place you have ever visited or would like to visit? What do you like about it?

2 What would be the perfect job for you after you have finished school and are out on your own?

Opening the Bible

What's Happened

God completes his six days of creation with a day of rest (2:1–3). But the narrator has not said everything he wishes about the creation of the human race in chapter 1, so he continues with a second account. The first account highlights humans' exalted status by setting our creation last: we are the summit of creation. The second account makes the same point in the opposite way, by placing the creation of humans before that of other living things. The first account indicates that we are made for a relationship with God by saying that we are in his image and likeness. The second account makes this point by showing the personal care with which God fashions and breathes life into man and woman.

THE READING

Genesis 2:4–25

The First Man

²⁴ These are the generations of the heavens and the earth when they were created.

In the day that the LORD God made the earth and the heavens, ⁵ when no plant of the field was yet in the earth and no herb of the field had yet sprung up—for the LORD God had not caused it to rain upon the earth, and there was no one to till the ground; ⁶ but a stream would rise from the earth, and water the whole face of the ground—⁷ then the LORD God formed man from the dust of the ground,* and breathed into his nostrils the breath of life; and the man became a living being. ⁸ And the LORD God planted a garden in Eden, in the east; and there he put the man whom he had formed. ⁹ Out of the ground the LORD God made to grow every tree that is pleasant to the sight and good for food, the tree of life also in the midst of the garden, and the tree of the knowledge of good and evil.

---

* The Hebrew word for man/mankind/human being (*adam*) sounds like the word for ground (*adamah*).

¹⁰ A river flows out of Eden to water the garden, and from there it divides and becomes four branches. ¹¹ The name of the first is Pishon; it is the one that flows around the whole land of Havilah, where there is gold; ¹² and the gold of that land is good; bdellium and onyx stone are there. ¹³ The name of the second river is Gihon; it is the one that flows around the whole land of Cush. ¹⁴ The name of the third river is Tigris, which flows east of Assyria. And the fourth river is the Euphrates.

Madam, I'm Adam

¹⁵ The LORD God took the man and put him in the garden of Eden to till it and keep it. ¹⁶ And the LORD God commanded the man, "You may freely eat of every tree of the garden; ¹⁷ but of the tree of the knowledge of good and evil you shall not eat, for in the day that you eat of it you shall die."

¹⁸ Then the LORD God said, "It is not good that the man should be alone; I will make him a helper as his partner." ¹⁹ So out of the ground the LORD God formed every animal of the field and every bird of the air, and brought them to the man to see what he would call them; and whatever the man called every living creature, that was its name. ²⁰ The man gave names to all cattle, and to the birds of the air, and to every animal of the field; but for the man there was not found a helper as his partner. ²¹ So the LORD God caused a deep sleep to fall upon the man, and he slept; then he took one of his ribs and closed up its place with flesh. ²² And the rib that the LORD God had taken from the man he made into a woman and brought her to the man. ²³ Then the man said,

> "This at last is bone of my bones
>   and flesh of my flesh;
> this one shall be called Woman,
>   for out of Man this one was taken."*

²⁴ Therefore a man leaves his father and his mother and clings to his wife, and they become one flesh. ²⁵ And the man and his wife were both naked, and were not ashamed.

---

* The Hebrew word for woman (*ishshah*) sounds like the word for man/adult male (*ish*).

Questions for a Closer Look

1 In chapter 1 God gives names to the basic components of the world. In chapter 2 the man gives names to the living creatures. What does this tell us about human beings?

2 What do verses 8–9 and 19–20 suggest about God's purpose for the plants and animals on the earth?

3 Verses 23 and 24 are linked by the word *therefore*. What is the narrator trying to explain? How would you clarify the explanation to someone who asked your help in understanding it?

4 How is the creation account in chapter 2 different from the account in chapter 1? What different points do the two accounts emphasize? Do the two accounts give a somewhat different picture of God?

A Guide to the Reading

God forms a human being from the ground (2:7). The narrator does not encourage us to picture how God creates the first human. The account does not speak of God literally using hands to mold the human figure. The man is formed from dust—hardly suitable material for molding. The actual process of human creation is left shrouded in mystery.

The account stresses the lofty dignity of human beings. Even though we consist of ordinary material elements, we have received our life directly from God. He has brought us into existence in, and for, a face-to-face relationship with him (2:7).

God plants an orchard to nourish the man (2:8–9). Eden is not a resort: the man is assigned to take care of it (2:15). He is going to have to work. Exercising "dominion" over the earth (1:26) requires effort. But of itself work is a gift, not a curse.

Two trees stand out (2:9). One is the tree of life. Apparently humans were not made immune to death. We needed something to sustain our lives. God intended that we would not die, but this was to be accomplished through eating the fruit of the tree of life. Saint Augustine regards this tree as a kind of sacrament. He writes that the tree of life would enable humans to draw strength, until eventually God would transform them and, without death, enable them to enter heaven.

We will leave the discussion of the tree of the knowledge of good and evil until next week. It is clear, however, that the man is limited by being forbidden to eat its fruit. To be a creature is to have limits. Yet God is not preoccupied with limits. He gives the man work; he grants him broad freedom in picking fruit (2:15–16). God is not predominantly a naysayer. Unfortunately, many people think of this story in terms of what God prohibits, failing to give sufficient attention to what God allows and what God calls the man to be and to do.

The man cannot live a truly human life by himself. He needs community. God wishes him to have "a helper as his partner" (2:18). The Hebrew word translated "helper" is not a servant word like *waiter* or *caterer.* It simply means "help." Usually it refers to

God or God's help, as in Psalm 121:1–2: "I lift up my eyes to the hills—from where will my *help* come? My *help* comes from the Lord who made heaven and earth" [italics mine].

God wants the man to have a helper "as his partner," or "corresponding to him." Together the words *help* and *partner* could be rendered "a helper who is his true counterpart." This implies sexual complementarity. God envisions a companion for the man in facing the practical necessities of life. The companion is to be a helper, not just now and then but throughout life, since this companion will be joined to him as a spouse (his true counterpart).

Searching for such a creature, God makes animals and brings them to the man to see if any of them might serve as a partner. (Who says there's no humor in the Bible?) By naming the animals, the man completes the name-giving that God left unfinished in chapter 1. This is the first exercise of the human role as God's representative. But none of the animals is an appropriate life companion for the man (2:19–20).

Most of the Genesis accounts are similar to stories told by Israel's neighbors. But 2:18–24 is the only account of the creation of woman known from the ancient Near East. The story expresses a high valuation of women: woman, taken from man, is man's equal.

The image of woman taken from man speaks about man's and woman's deep-rooted drive for union with each other. The story indicates that when man and woman are drawn together in marriage, they fulfill the destiny for which God created them. In the ancient world, property and status strongly influenced decisions about who married whom, yet these are not identified here as reasons for marriage. The account puts the accent on man's and woman's attraction to each other, dramatically expressed in the man's delighted recognition of the woman (2:23). Remarkably, not even offspring are mentioned here as a reason for marriage (that was covered in 1:28). There is a clear suggestion that marriage is based on the power of love between man and woman, and that God is the source of that power.

Questions for Application

1 Do you think everyone gets lonely at times? How can you tell when someone is lonely? What can you do for someone who is lonely?

2 How has your work as a student been a blessing for you? In what ways has it been a mixed blessing?

3 Have you watched as God provided something good to a person close to you? What effect might this have had on his or her relationship with God?

4 To whom do young people usually turn for help and companionship? What are the best ways to show love in those relationships?

Approach to Prayer

Call to mind your friends. Take some time to reflect on those who feel as though they have no friends.

Listen as someone prays this prayer aloud:

Father, thank you providing us with friends, those companions and helpers who are always present when we need them. Bless them and let them experience your immense love in their lives. Bless also all those who are lonely: may they soon discover the joy of friendship. Finally, Father, bless all the married women and men who are providing help and companionship to each other.

If you wish, offer a short, spontaneous prayer along this line. Then listen as other members of the group pray this prayer:

Lord, thank you for being the ultimate helper of our lives. You are the companion who never abandons or neglects us. Show your presence and love to all those who are lonely.

End by praying the Our Father with the group.

A Living Tradition

A Saint Who Found Genesis Hard to Understand

Saint Augustine, a North African bishop who died in 425, was one of the greatest thinkers in the history of the Church. Yet for more than 30 years he labored to understand Genesis and still had questions. Augustine wrote a commentary on Genesis soon after his adult conversion, but he was unhappy with it. He tried writing another interpretation a few years later but gave up before finishing the book. "I collapsed under the weight of a burden I could not bear," he said later. Eventually Augustine wrote a third commentary. It took him 14 years.

Augustine showed intellectual humility in his approach to Genesis, acknowledging that "we do not know that which is so far outside our experience." He was always open to better interpretations than his own. "If anyone is of the opinion that this passage should be explained differently and he is able to lay out a more likely interpretation," Augustine wrote, "not only should I not resist him, I should thank him."

Keenly aware of the limits of his knowledge, Augustine was wary of arguing too strongly for his own views. In fact, he did not like arguing at all. "It is better to admit that we are in doubt regarding obscure things than to argue over them," he wrote. "Such things are perhaps just barely discovered by those who seek calmly, never by those striving contentiously."

Not surprisingly, Augustine constantly reminded his readers that God's help is indispensable for understanding Genesis. Augustine said he did not know how much the Lord was going to help him in his commentary, but he knew one thing for sure: "Unless the Lord helps, I am not going to speak rightly!"

Augustine would be a good model to follow as you struggle to understand Genesis. Like Augustine, try to be humble and not think that yours is the only way to interpret the stories of Genesis. Like Augustine, do not get caught up in pointless arguments about the interpretation of stories. And like Augustine, rely on God's help in listening to the stories and deciding what they might mean and how they might apply to your life.

Between Discussions

The hope of eternal happiness with God after earthly life spread gradually among Jews in the Old Testament period. As it did, Jews began to look back to the garden in Eden as an image of final bliss. It seemed reasonable to think that the happiness that God would grant at the end of the world would resemble the happiness he granted at the beginning. In their reflections they sometimes used the term *Paradise*—a Persian word meaning "a walled park of trees"—to refer to Eden and, by extension, to eternal life with God.

Jewish rabbis reflected on the nature of paradise. One ancient description portrays a paradise consisting of five chambers for various classes of the righteous. The chambers differ in their makeup—the first one, for example, is made of cedar with a transparent crystal ceiling, while the third chamber is built of silver and gold, ornamented with pearls, and filled with spices, fragrance, and sweet odors. A later rabbinic account describes arrival in paradise: hundreds of thousands of angels wait at diamond-studded gates to welcome the righteous, who are crowned and dressed royally. Once in paradise, the righteous feast with God and David and the rest of the righteous.

The Muslim paradise tends to be filled with wonderful delights: silk and comfortable couches, pleasant weather, tasty fruits, ginger-flavored drink, and most important, at the center of everything, flowing water. The righteous in paradise will have every desirable pleasure, and all their wishes will be granted. And yet, none of these satisfactions will come close to equaling the delight of seeing God's face.

Christian portrayals of paradise have been based on the Genesis account. Already in the early Church the garden of Eden was considered as providing a glimpse of the happiness of heaven (2 Corinthians 12:1–4). Some of the Fathers of the Church took up this line of reflection, among them a fourth-century Syrian deacon named Ephrem. His *Hymns of Paradise* is one of the most beautiful writings of the early Church.

In the hymns, Saint Ephrem pictures Eden as a lush park at the top of a mountain—an interpretation modern scholars affirm, for *Eden* means "luxuriant," and the garden seems to have been on a hilltop, from which springwaters rushed down to the rest of the world (2:10–14). In his description of Eden, however, Ephrem enlarges imaginatively on the text. For Ephrem, the beauty of Eden expresses a key principle: no matter how much effort is involved on our part, the journey to God is fundamentally a matter of our yielding to God's attraction. He regards the text of Genesis as an invitation to taste the delights of God's love. In his own meditations on paradise, Ephrem felt enriched and intoxicated, forgetting about his poverty and his sins.

In the final analysis, we must keep in mind what the *Catechism of the Catholic Church* says about paradise: "This mystery of blessed communion with God and all who are in Christ is beyond all understanding and description. Scripture speaks of it in images: life, light, peace, wedding feast, wine of the kingdom, the Father's house, the heavenly Jerusalem, paradise: 'no eye has seen, nor ear heard, nor the heart of man conceived, what God has prepared for those who love him' (1 Corinthians 2:9)."

Distrust, Disobedience, and Dismay

Warm-Up Questions

1 What types of punishments do parents generally use? Do they tend to be effective? What are punishments able, and unable, to accomplish with children and teenagers?

2 What are some of the biggest limitations on the lives of young people?

Opening the Bible

Genesis 3:1–24

Temptation and Fall

3:1 Now the serpent was more crafty than any other wild animal that the LORD God had made. He said to the woman, "Did God say, 'You shall not eat from any tree in the garden'?" 2 The woman said to the serpent, "We may eat of the fruit of the trees in the garden; 3 but God said, 'You shall not eat of the fruit of the tree that is in the middle of the garden, nor shall you touch it, or you shall die.'" 4 But the serpent said to the woman, "You will not die; 5 for God knows that when you eat of it your eyes will be opened, and you will be like God, knowing good and evil." 6 So when the woman saw that the tree was good for food, and that it was a delight to the eyes, and that the tree was to be desired to make one wise, she took of its fruit and ate; and she also gave some to her husband, who was with her, and he ate. 7 Then the eyes of both were opened, and they knew that they were naked; and they sewed fig leaves together and made loincloths for themselves.

8 They heard the sound of the LORD God walking in the garden at the time of the evening breeze, and the man and his wife hid themselves from the presence of the LORD God among the trees of the garden. 9 But the LORD God called to the man, and said to him, "Where are you?" 10 He said, "I heard the sound of you in the garden, and I was afraid, because I was naked; and I hid myself." 11 He said, "Who told you that you were naked? Have you eaten from the tree of which I commanded you not to eat?" 12 The man said, "The woman whom you gave to be with me, she gave me fruit from the tree, and I ate." 13 Then the LORD God said to the woman, "What is this that you have done?" The woman said, "The serpent tricked me, and I ate." 14 The LORD God said to the serpent,

> "Because you have done this,
>> cursed are you among all animals
>> and among all wild creatures;
> upon your belly you shall go,
>> and dust you shall eat
>> all the days of your life.

[15] I will put enmity between you and the woman,
    and between your offspring and hers;
  he will strike your head,
    and you will strike his heel."
[16] To the woman he said,
    "I will greatly increase your pangs in childbearing;
      in pain you shall bring forth children,
    yet your desire shall be for your husband,
      and he shall rule over you."
[17] And to the man he said,
    "Because you have listened to the voice of your wife,
      and have eaten of the tree
    about which I commanded you,
      'You shall not eat of it,'
    cursed is the ground because of you;
      in toil you shall eat of it all the days of your life;
[18] thorns and thistles it shall bring forth for you;
      and you shall eat the plants of the field.
[19] By the sweat of your face
    you shall eat bread
  until you return to the ground,
    for out of it you were taken;
  you are dust,
    and to dust you shall return."

[20] The man named his wife Eve,* because she was the mother of all living. [21] And the LORD God made garments of skins for the man and for his wife, and clothed them.

[22] Then the LORD God said, "See, the man has become like one of us, knowing good and evil; and now, he might reach out his hand and take also from the tree of life, and eat, and live forever"—[23] therefore the LORD God sent him forth from the garden of Eden, to till the ground from which he was taken. [24] He drove out the man; and at the east of the garden of Eden he placed the cherubim, and a sword flaming and turning to guard the way to the tree of life.

---

* In Hebrew, Eve's name resembles the word for living.

Questions for a Closer Look

1 Compare what God says in 2:16–17 with the snake's quotation in 3:1. How does the snake misquote God? What is the effect of the snake's misquotation?

2 The woman does not quote God exactly, either (3:3). What does she add? What effect does her addition have on the picture of God that she conveys?

3 Why would the woman believe what the snake says in 3:4–5?

4 Verse 6 describes how the fruit of the tree of the knowledge of good and evil appears to Eve. How is this fruit different from the fruit of the other trees (see 2:9)? If the fruit of the other trees is also pleasant and nutritious, why is Eve now especially attracted to this one?

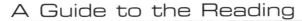

A Guide to the Reading

The first puzzle in this reading is the snake. How did an adversary of God get into the garden, and why did it mislead the woman? The narrator does not make the snake the focus of attention, probably to avoid shifting the responsibility for disobeying God away from the man and woman.

A greater puzzle is the tree "in the middle of the garden" (3:3)—the tree of the knowledge of good and evil. What does it mean? Saint Clement of Alexandria thought that the "knowledge of good and evil" represents sexual intercourse. Saint Augustine disagreed, pointing out that there was nothing to forbid the man and the woman from having intercourse if they wished. Some have proposed that the tree represents the ability to tell right from wrong. But God's instruction in 2:17 assumes that the man and the woman can already grasp that it is wrong to eat the fruit.

Later God says that he himself possesses the knowledge of good and evil (3:22), so this knowledge must be sinful only for human beings. Apparently it means making up your own mind about what will be helpful or harmful for you. Eating from this tree represents taking mastery over your own life—a mastery that rightfully belongs to God. That is why the snake says that eating the fruit makes you "like God" (3:5): it gives you a divine ability to have complete control over your existence.

The woman sees that the fruit is "good" (3:6). What irony! The *creator* knows what is good and has provided it for human beings (1:4,31; 2:18), but now the woman goes against the Creator's instructions and decides for herself what is good. She sees that the fruit will make her "wise"; the Hebrew could also be translated "successful." The woman thinks that if she eats the fruit she will know how to run her own life successfully apart from God. What folly!

The woman hands the fruit to her husband, who is "with her" (3:6). Apparently he has been silently present throughout the conversation. The narrator does not report any attempt by the woman to persuade her husband. Perhaps he has reached his own decision to eat the fruit, based on what he has heard the snake say.

Before eating the fruit, the couple cannot fully understand why it is forbidden. A command that cannot be fully understood raises the issue of trust. A person keeps such a command only because he or she hears in it the voice of the one who commands. God's command gives the first humans the opportunity to trust him. They choose instead to suspect that he does not have their best interests at heart. This lack of trust in God, with the claim to be master of one's own life apart from God, is the root of sin. Uprooting it will require a perfect act of trust in God, a total abandonment of self to God: Jesus' death on a cross.

Eating the fruit shatters the harmony between man and woman and between the couple and God (3:7–8). This is the origin of the moral disorder and broken relationship with God that we are born into—the condition called original sin.

The woman and the man have turned away from their creator, the source of life. Their lives, then, are poisoned at the source. The woman's source is the man. She should experience peace and fulfillment in her relationship with him, but now that relationship will be marred by oppression (3:16). The man's source is the ground. Now this relationship is also disturbed: farming will involve backbreaking toil (3:17–19). The same Hebrew word is used for the woman's pain in childbirth and the man's pain in his work. Adam and Eve suffer different, but equal, penalties.

God had warned them about the tree of the knowledge of good and evil, "In the day that you eat of it you shall die" (2:17). This amounted to a death sentence, equivalent to "You will surely be put to death." Eating the fruit was a capital offense. Now that the man and the woman have violated their relationship with God, God seals off the tree of life (3:22–24). The man and the woman no longer have access to the divine power that would have preserved them against the forces of disintegration. Eventually they will die.

Questions for Application

1 Why are people often attracted to things simply because they are forbidden? What can a person do to resist that attraction?

2 In your experience, do young people tend to blame others for their faults?

3 How can we avoid doing things that seem attractive and reasonable at the time but don't make as much sense after we have done them?

4 How does trusting God help us make the right moral decisions?

5 When do you think it is hardest for people to trust in God's care for them? What is the best way to express trust in God?

Approach to Prayer

With the group, express your desire to trust and be obedient toward God by praying two psalms that express trust in God: Psalm 90 and Psalm 131. In an encounter with Satan, Jesus exemplified the absolute trust in God that Psalm 90 speaks of (Luke 4:9–13). Psalm 131 gives voice to childlike trust in God and an acceptance of creaturely limitations.

A Living Tradition

An Affectionate Father

Around the year 385 Saint John Chrysostom gave a series of talks on Genesis in the cathedral parish in Antioch (present-day south central Turkey). John encouraged the laypeople who came to study the Bible with him to see a tenderhearted God in Genesis 3.

John compared God to "an affectionate father who sees his own child dragged down from respectability to the most squalid circumstances by carelessly doing things that are unworthy of his noble birth. Out of warmhearted, fatherly compassion he cannot bear to let his child remain in that condition but wishes to free him from his squalor little by little and bring him back to his original honor." Thus, John said, when Adam and Eve sin, God wastes no time. That very afternoon he goes looking for them in the garden (3:8).

When God calls out to Adam (3:9), John surmised that Adam is tongue-tied in his shame, yet God gives him the opportunity to explain himself (3:11). "See the Lord's love for humans, his extravagant forbearance. He is able to punish such a great sinner at once. But he patiently restrains himself and asks him questions, virtually inviting a defense." To John, God seems more disappointed than angry. He imagined God saying to Adam, "Surely I didn't cramp your enjoyment? Didn't I provide you with abundance and put you in charge of everything in Paradise? Didn't I command you to keep away from just this *one* thing?"

John acknowledged that in the end God imposes penalties on Adam and Eve, but even in their punishments he saw signs of God's mercy. The woman's pain in childbirth is softened by the joy of the baby who follows, and the hard work will remind the man that he needs to humble himself before God.

As a loving parent, God has challenged his children to do better by forcing them to deal with the unpleasant consequences of their decisions.

I f you ever pass through Jericho, a city near the Jordan River, be sure to see the *tel*. A tel is an artificial hill consisting of layer upon layer of ruins. A tel was produced in ancient times as one group of people after another lived on a site. Each group would level the buildings of the previous one and build on top. Over the course of centuries, as new levels were added, the town would rise higher and higher. The result is an archaeological wedding cake composed of layers from successive periods. The tel in Jericho is remarkable because Jericho is the longest continuously occupied human site in the world. Looking down a shaft cut through the tel, you can see walls constructed more than 9,000 years ago.

We might compare the Bible to a tel. The levels of the biblical tel are composed not of ruined buildings but of layers of meaning, built up through stages of composition and interpretation. The biblical tel contains many levels of meaning, since the Bible passed through many centuries of writing and editing, then through more centuries of study and reflection.

An example of the multileveled meaning of the Genesis text is the least-appealing participant in the drama of chapter 3: the snake. Over more than 3,000 years, the snake has passed through at least five stages of understanding, making it a richly meaningful, while always unpleasant, character.

At the bottom layer of the tel, so to speak, are pre-Israelite myths—stories of origin bearing a religious meaning. During the pre-Israelite period, ancient Near Eastern people regarded snakes with both awe and dread. The Egyptians put carvings of snakes on the pharaoh's crown, as an expression of divine protection. Snakes were used in various tales to symbolize divine and demonic powers.

The next level of meaning was provided by the Israelite author. He drew elements from stories of the older, polytheistic culture to weave his accounts of creation and fall. But the narrator campaigned *against* the idea that snakes are divine or demonic. He emphasized that snakes are simply snakes. In stating that the snake is one of the animals "that the LORD God had made" (3:1), he is making it clear that the snake is not a god. The snake has no spiritual power; it is merely clever. The Genesis narrator wanted his readers to see that there is only one God, who has created everything; the world is not filled with many gods. He wants them to understand that our unhappiness is brought on not by mean-spirited gods or demons, as Israel's neighbors thought, but by bad choices.

A third level of meaning developed among Jews in the century or so before Christ. Understanding the role of angels in the world, they saw that some angels had refused to serve God's purposes. The leader of these rebellious spirits, called the devil, then sought to disrupt God's relationship with his human creatures. The Jewish thinkers reread the Genesis account and recognized the snake as a mouthpiece for this leader in his diabolical attempt to bring humans to ruin (Wisdom 2:24).

Christians added to the Biblical tel with their belief that Christ has now overcome the devil by his death and resurrection. They read God's declaration that there would be hostility between the snake's offspring and the woman's offspring (3:15), and they detected in it the first hint that God's Son, born as a human being, would break the grip of the devil over human beings.

Another layer of meaning has developed recently. Modern psychology might help us see the snake as a symbol of some of our darker unconscious drives. The conversation between the snake and the woman might be read as an expression of an inner confrontation between selfish desires and the awareness of moral demands.

While the levels of meaning in the Bible resemble a tel, they are unlike a tel in an important respect. People lived only on the top level of the tel. At each stage, the previous levels lay hidden and inaccessible. This is not the case, however, with the Bible. We can understand, appreciate, and learn from all the levels of meaning that have accumulated in the course of its composition and use. We are the heirs of a rich tradition, a tradition guided by God in both its writing and its interpretation.

East of Eden

Warm-Up Questions

1 Which of these technological innovations do you appreciate most: DVD players, cell phones, the Internet, CD burners, GPS receivers?

2 What are the advantages of having children when you are younger, say around 20? What are the advantages of having children when you are older, say around 35?

Opening the Bible

Genesis 4:1—5:5

Envy, Murder, and Judgment

^{4:1} Now the man knew his wife Eve, and she conceived and bore Cain, saying, "I have produced a man with the help of the LORD." ² Next she bore his brother Abel. Now Abel was a keeper of sheep, and Cain a tiller of the ground. ³ In the course of time Cain brought to the LORD an offering of the fruit of the ground, ⁴ and Abel for his part brought of the firstlings of his flock, their fat portions. And the LORD had regard for Abel and his offering, ⁵ but for Cain and his offering he had no regard. So Cain was very angry, and his countenance fell. ⁶ The LORD said to Cain, "Why are you angry, and why has your countenance fallen? ⁷ If you do well, will you not be accepted? And if you do not do well, sin is lurking at the door; its desire is for you, but you must master it."

⁸ Cain said to his brother Abel, "Let us go out to the field." And when they were in the field, Cain rose up against his brother Abel, and killed him. ⁹ Then the LORD said to Cain, "Where is your brother Abel?" He said, "I do not know; am I my brother's keeper?" ¹⁰ And the LORD said, "What have you done? Listen; your brother's blood is crying out to me from the ground! ¹¹ And now you are cursed from the ground, which has opened its mouth to receive your brother's blood from your hand. ¹² When you till the ground, it will no longer yield to you its strength; you will be a fugitive and a wanderer on the earth." ¹³ Cain said to the LORD, "My punishment is greater than I can bear! ¹⁴ Today you have driven me away from the soil, and I shall be hidden from your face; I shall be a fugitive and a wanderer on the earth, and anyone who meets me may kill me." ¹⁵ Then the LORD said to him, "Not so! Whoever kills Cain will suffer a sevenfold vengeance." And the LORD put a mark on Cain, so that no one who came upon him would kill him. ¹⁶ Then Cain went away from the presence of the LORD, and settled in the land of Nod, east of Eden.

A Clever but Ruthless Family

[17] Cain knew his wife, and she conceived and bore Enoch; and he built a city, and named it Enoch after his son Enoch. [18] To Enoch was born Irad; and Irad was the father of Mehujael, and Mehujael the father of Methushael, and Methushael the father of Lamech. [19] Lamech took two wives; the name of the one was Adah, and the name of the other Zillah. [20] Adah bore Jabal; he was the ancestor of those who live in tents and have livestock. [21] His brother's name was Jubal; he was the ancestor of all those who play the lyre and pipe. [22] Zillah bore Tubal-cain, who made all kinds of bronze and iron tools. The sister of Tubal-cain was Naamah.

[23] Lamech said to his wives:
"Adah and Zillah, hear my voice;
        you wives of Lamech, listen to what I say:
I have killed a man for wounding me,
        a young man for striking me.
[24] If Cain is avenged sevenfold,
        truly Lamech seventy-sevenfold."

Adam and Eve Carry On

[25] Adam knew his wife again, and she bore a son and named him Seth, for she said, "God has appointed for me another child instead of Abel, because Cain killed him." [26] To Seth also a son was born, and he named him Enosh. At that time people began to invoke the name of the LORD.

[5:1] This is the list of the descendants of Adam. When God created humankind, he made them in the likeness of God. [2] Male and female he created them, and he blessed them and named them "Humankind" when they were created.

[3] When Adam had lived one hundred thirty years, he became the father of a son in his likeness, according to his image, and named him Seth. [4] The days of Adam after he became the father of Seth were eight hundred years; and he had other sons and daughters. [5] Thus all the days that Adam lived were nine hundred thirty years; and he died.

Questions for a Closer Look

1 How does Cain's response to God (4:9) compare to his father's response (3:10,12)? How is Cain like his father? How is he different?

2 Reread 3:21 and 4:15. What do they suggest about God's relationship with sinners?

3 Why doesn't Cain express repentance? Why don't Adam and Eve express repentance?

4 Compare 3:2–6 and 4:6–8. How does the narrator show that Adam, Eve, and Cain were responsible for their actions?

5 What do Jesus' words in Matthew 18:21–22 suggest about his view of Lamech's words in Genesis 4:23–24?

A Guide to the Reading

Adam and Eve have intercourse, and Eve bears a son (4:1). Eve declares that she has "produced" a man with the help of the Lord; the Hebrew word may be translated "created" (as in Proverbs 8:22). Despite their banishment from the garden of Eden, in begetting new human beings, man and woman are cocreators with God—an awesome privilege. Eve calls God "the LORD" using God's proper name in the Old Testament (Hebrew "Yahweh"). Notably it is a woman who first utters this name, so sacred in Jewish tradition that later it came almost never to be spoken.

Conflict arises between the first two brothers when God accepts Abel's offering but not Cain's (4:3–5). The narrator does not tell us why God rejects Cain's offering. Perhaps Cain has done something wrong. Or this may be the first of many biblical episodes in which God, for reasons known only to him, favors a younger son over an older one (for example, Joseph over his brothers—Genesis 37:1–11). The acceptance of Abel's offering and the rejection of Cain's may thus represent situations where people for some reason are not equal. Like all of us, Cain is tempted to envy what seems like God's better treatment of someone else.

God compares Cain's temptation to a beast crouching to spring (4:7), a vivid image of the destructive power of envy and rage. We have been created to rule the world (1:28), but we must first decide whether to rule ourselves.

Cain chooses not to. Consequently the first death comes not from natural causes but by human hands. In response, God imposes a severe penalty (4:12): ancient people considered banishment to be as harsh a punishment as death.

Cain protests. He senses that God is compassionate, so he tries to move God to lighten the sentence (4:13–14). This appeal is the first prayer of petition in the Bible, made by a man guilty of murder, and God hears it! Thus the episode contains both the cry of Abel's blood and the lament of his killer, and God heeds them both. It is obvious that God is never far away from us, no matter what situation we find ourselves in.

Driven away from God because of his crime, Cain yet remains in God's care. Cain's life, no less than Abel's, belongs to God. To deter anyone from avenging Abel's murder, God puts a mark on Cain (4:15). Since this mark identifies him as a killer, it is a mark of shame, but chiefly it is a safeguard, showing that God remains Cain's protector. The narrator does not say what the mark is. It may have been a mark on the forehead. Early Jewish rabbis, living in a culture that considered dogs no better than rats, suggested that the mark that God gave Cain was a dog as a companion.

Cain and his descendants develop the rudiments of civilization and urban life (4:17–22). There are seven generations from Adam through Cain to Lamech, just as there were seven days of creation. In other words, when we cultivate and develop the earth, we are co-workers with God, made in his image. The fact that technology is produced by *Cain's* descendants does not diminish its goodness. But God-given intelligence is now being used by a race that often rejects God's purposes.

Cain's descendant Lamech boasts of exacting blood vengeance, the very thing against which God protected Cain (4:24). It shows how irrational revenge is, for if people had done to Cain what Lamech does to his enemies, Cain would have been killed and Lamech would never have existed. The span from Cain to Lamech marks a descent into violence. Yet the race is not utterly corrupt. Brutal Lamech has a daughter called Naamah—a Hebrew name that means "pleasant" or "dear" (4:22). Perhaps her charming mother has something to do with this; *Zillah* may mean "melody" (4:19).

Returning to Adam and Eve, the narrator tells us that they continue to have children, who are also made in the divine image (5:3). Despite our sins, we continue to bear the dignity of being in God's likeness; we continue to exist for the purpose of a relationship with God. Our final verse (5:5) records the tragedy that has befallen Adam and all his descendants: earthly death.

Questions for Application

1 Some people have more talents than others. Some have lower IQs. Some are born healthy, while others are not. Is God fair? Is he just?

2 What is wrong with envy? From your own experience, what are the results of envy?

3 When is it OK to get angry at someone in your family, and when is it wrong? How can you tell the difference?

4 How might people be tempted to misuse the technology that is at their disposal (machinery, appliances, electronics)? How can they avoid such misuse?

5 In what ways can the desire for revenge poison a person's life? What are some things we can do to express forgiveness and love when we are tempted to seek revenge?

Approach to Prayer

Pray along with the group this portion of a prayer by Saint Francis of Assisi:

Lord, make me an instrument
of your peace. Where there is
hatred, let me sow love; where
there is injury, let me sow pardon.
Where there is darkness, let me
give light; where there
is sadness, let me give joy.

O divine Master, grant that I
may not try to be comforted, but
to comfort; not try to be loved,
but to love.

Because it is in giving that we are
received; it is in forgiving that we
are forgiven; and it is in dying
that we are born to eternal life.

Saints in the Making

Light over the Scaffold

On February 25, 1954, 23-year-old Jacques Fesch beat and robbed an elderly broker in an office in the financial district of Paris. Fesch hoped to buy a boat with the money. When the victim's cries attracted attention, Fesch fled into the street, pursued by a policeman named George Vergnes. After a brief chase, Vergnes closed in on Fesch and shouted to him to surrender. In panic Fesch turned, pulled a gun from his overcoat, and shot Vergnes through the heart, killing him instantly. Fesch was captured minutes later at a nearby subway station.

Fesch was interrogated and placed in solitary confinement until his trial. The prison chaplain came to see him, but at first Fesch was not interested in talking with him.

In solitude Fesch tried to understand his own actions. The robbery had been his first crime. Fesch began to see himself with great clarity. "During the years when I lived without faith," he wrote, "I did evil, much evil, less through deliberate malice than through heedlessness, egoism, and hardness of heart. I was incapable of loving anyone." Fesch realized that the robbery and murder were the "logical consequence of all the evil seething" within him.

After several months' imprisonment, Fesch had an experience of grace. "A powerful wave of emotion swept over me, causing deep and brutal suffering," he wrote. "Within the space of a few hours I came into possession of faith."

With the help of the prison chaplain, his lawyer, and a monk who wrote to him, the young prisoner began a journey toward God. During the three years that stretched out from his conversion to his execution, Fesch sat alone in his cell. He prayed, read, reflected on his life, and wrote letters, which revealed his repentance and a deepening honesty. Humility began to replace egoism. Fesch told his mother that, corresponding with the monk, "I feel like a raccoon trying to carry on a conversation with a dove in the clouds. . . . If he could ever see into the recesses of my soul!"

In his final letter, written the morning of his execution, he expressed both overwhelming fear and supreme confidence in Christ's promise of forgiveness and eternal life.

Between Discussions

Adam and Eve overstep the limit that God set for them, trying to make themselves masters of their own lives (chapter 3). Chapter 4 shows the unhappy effects of this choice on their children and descendants. From Cain to Lamech, the human race goes from bad to worse.

These early chapters of Genesis also show God holding steady to his purposes in the face of human decline. At the beginning God put the blessing of fertility within us and gave us the capacity to rule the earth (1:28). It is clear from Eve's joy at the birth of her first child and the technological and artistic creativity of the Cain family (4:1,20–22) that God has not withdrawn his gifts. We get the picture of a God who never stops looking for ways to accomplish his purposes with his beloved human creatures, flawed as they are. God generously blesses us with our lives, our sexuality, our talents, and our resources, and then he patiently waits to see whether we will make good use of them.

God's punishments seem harsh, but they do not give us the whole picture of what God is like. Genesis is part of a gradual revelation of God to the community of faith. Even in these early stories, the narrator portrays a God who is concerned with justice, unlike the gods of Israel's neighbors. For example, the narrator shows God fitting the punishment to the crime. For tempting the woman to eat forbidden fruit, the snake is condemned to eat dust; for committing a sin by eating, the man is punished by difficulty in obtaining food (3:14,17–19). The ground that drank Abel's blood will no longer yield crops for his murderer (4:11–12). God does not dream up arbitrary punishments, as the gods of Israel's neighbors would have done, but rather matches the punishment with the crime.

The poetic justice in these accounts shows that God created the world with a moral order, and violations of that order bring painful consequences. Sin cannot bring lasting happiness because it runs counter to the design of creation. So in one sense, the punishments for sin in Genesis are personal judgments by God.

But in another sense, they are the built-in results of tampering with the order that God has created.

God is patient in his dealings with humans even as he punishes them. He sentences Adam and Eve, then gives them longer-lasting clothing to replace the fig-leaf loincloths they hurriedly stitched together (3:7,21). He condemns Cain to a life of wandering, then puts his protection on him (4:15).

The narrator tells us that Seth has a son named Enosh (4:26). Both the name *Adam* and the name *Enosh* mean "human," but they have different connotations. *Adam* echoes the word for ground—the ground from which he is taken, which he is assigned to cultivate, and to which he will return (2:7,15; 3:17,19). *Enosh* is related to a word meaning "weak" or "frail." It is interesting to note that at the time of the birth of Enosh "people began to invoke the name of the LORD " (4:26). The narrator seems to suggest that as people became aware of their weaknesses as human beings, they realized their need for God and instinctively turned towards prayer. The "name of the LORD " is Yahweh, the personal name of God in the Hebrew Bible. The woman, Eve, first utters this personal name of God (4:1), but not in prayer, as Enosh had done (4:26).

The notice that "at that time people began to invoke the name of the LORD" is interesting in another way. In the biblical story, God does not reveal his personal name until later, when he speaks to Moses from the burning bush (Exodus 3:15). But the Genesis narrator shows his awareness that even before God began to unfold his plan of salvation through the people of Israel, he made himself present to men and women. God does the same with people today, making himself present to people whether or not they know about his supreme revelation of himself in his Son, Jesus Christ. As Saint Paul indicated to an audience in Athens, God is not far from any of us but calls all men and women, in every place and religion, to seek and find him (Acts 17:22–31).

God Starts Over

Warm-Up Questions

1 How did you learn to swim? If you have not learned to swim, what has held you back?

2 Have you ever watched as someone did the right thing despite the misguided attitudes or behavior of others around them? What did you learn from this situation?

Opening the Bible

What's Happened

Genesis continues with a genealogy tracing 10 generations from Adam (5:6–32), followed by fragmentary and very mysterious references to divine beings and giants (6:1–4). After this, the narrator takes up a much more familiar story: Noah and the flood.

THE READING

Genesis 6:5—9:11

A Disappointed Creator

⁶:⁵ The LORD saw that the wickedness of humankind was great in the earth, and that every inclination of the thoughts of their hearts was only evil continually. ⁶ And the LORD was sorry that he had made humankind on the earth, and it grieved him to his heart. ⁷ So the LORD said, "I will blot out from the earth the human beings I have created—people together with animals and creeping things and birds of the air, for I am sorry that I have made them." ⁸ But Noah found favor in the sight of the LORD. . . .

¹³ And God said to Noah, "I have determined to make an end of all flesh, for the earth is filled with violence because of them; now I am going to destroy them along with the earth. ¹⁴ Make yourself an ark of cypress wood; make rooms in the ark, and cover it inside and out with pitch. . . . ¹⁷ For my part, I am going to bring a flood of waters on the earth, to destroy from under heaven all flesh in which is the breath of life; everything that is on the earth shall die. ¹⁸ But I will establish my covenant with you; and you shall come into the ark, you, your sons, your wife, and your sons' wives with you. ¹⁹ And of every living thing, of all flesh, you shall bring two of every kind into the ark, to keep them alive with you; they shall be male and female. . . ." ²² Noah did this; he did all that God commanded him.

⁷:¹ Then the LORD said to Noah, "Go into the ark, you and all your household, for I have seen that you alone are righteous before me in this generation." . . . ¹¹ On that day all the fountains of the great deep burst forth, and the windows of the heavens were opened. . . . ¹⁷ The flood continued forty days on the earth; and the waters increased, and bore up the ark, and it rose high above the earth. . . . ¹⁹ The

waters swelled so mightily on the earth that all the high mountains under the whole heaven were covered. . . . [21] And all flesh died that moved on the earth, birds, domestic animals, wild animals, all swarming creatures that swarm on the earth, and all human beings. . . .

[8:1] But God remembered Noah and all the wild animals and all the domestic animals that were with him in the ark. And God made a wind blow over the earth . . . [2] the rain from the heavens was restrained, [3] and the waters gradually receded from the earth. . . . [18] So Noah went out with his sons and his wife and his sons' wives. . . .

A Fresh Start

[20] Then Noah built an altar to the LORD, and took of every clean animal and of every clean bird, and offered burnt offerings on the altar. [21] And when the LORD smelled the pleasing odor, the LORD said in his heart, "I will never again curse the ground because of humankind, for the inclination of the human heart is evil from youth; nor will I ever again destroy every living creature as I have done. . . ."

[9:1] God blessed Noah and his sons, and said to them, "Be fruitful and multiply, and fill the earth. [2] The fear and dread of you shall rest on every animal of the earth, and on every bird of the air, on everything that creeps on the ground, and on all the fish of the sea; into your hand they are delivered. [3] Every moving thing that lives shall be food for you; and just as I gave you the green plants, I give you everything. [4] Only, you shall not eat flesh with its life, that is, its blood. [5] For your own lifeblood I will surely require a reckoning: from every animal I will require it and from human beings, each one for the blood of another, I will require a reckoning for human life.

[6] Whoever sheds the blood of a human,
> by a human shall that person's blood be shed;
for in his own image
> God made humankind. . . .

[9] As for me, I am establishing my covenant with you and your descendants after you, [10] and with every living creature that is with you, the birds, the domestic animals, and every animal of the earth with you, as many as came out of the ark. [11] I establish my covenant with you, that never again shall all flesh be cut off by the waters of a flood, and never again shall there be a flood to destroy the earth."

Questions for a Closer Look

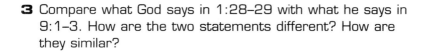

1 How would you describe God's reaction to human wickedness in 6:5–7?

2 Compare the description of humankind in 6:5 to the description in 8:21. How did the flood change people? Why? What kind of change in people is needed?

3 Compare what God says in 1:28–29 with what he says in 9:1–3. How are the two statements different? How are they similar?

4 In what ways do God's instructions to Noah in 9:1–6 show that he is making an accommodation for the condition of human beings described in 8:21?

A Guide to the Reading

The flood story is disturbing. God wipes out all but a handful of people. Boys playing, grandmothers baking bread, farmers plowing their fields—all are washed away without warning. Could they *all* have been so wicked (6:5,11–13) that they deserved to drown? We might be tempted to ask the question: Why didn't God send a prophet to warn people about the possibility of a flood? But such questions are unanswerable, and we should remember that none of these early chapters of Genesis presents literal accounts. The flood story, like many other stories in these first chapters of Genesis, is not history. It is closer to a parable than to a newspaper report. Whatever judgment God actually brought on the human race in the long ages of prehistory, the specific events are hidden from us now. To accept the story of the flood as teaching truths, we do not have to believe that God actually destroyed everyone with a flood, just as we can accept the creation story as teaching truths without holding that God created the world in six days.

The flood is such a drastic punishment for sin, it seems that God must have been angry. But the account never speaks of God's anger. It says he is "grieved"; it even tells us God is "sorry that he had made humankind" (6:6)—a bold way of expressing how thoroughly sickened God is at the sight of criminal violence and oppression (6:11,13). God comes across as an anguished parent, somewhat like a mother who sorrowfully tells the police where her son is after he has committed a crime.

The story may at first seem to focus on destruction, yet the doom of earth's inhabitants unfolds off camera without description (7:21–23). In the foreground of the picture is Noah and his family floating safely away, warned and carefully instructed by God. The accent is on salvation.

It is God, not skillful shipbuilding or plucky sailing, who saves Noah. The ark is an unwieldy houseboat—a rectangular box some 450 feet long, 75 feet wide, and 45 feet high (6:15). God shuts Noah in (7:16), and Noah cannot even see out, let alone steer (8:6–13). He is completely in God's hands.

In essence, the flood is a re-creation story. God undoes the first creation. He allows the waters of the ocean above the sky to pour down onto the earth and the waters under the earth to gush upward (7:11). The world returns to a condition of watery chaos (compare 1:2). Then God makes the human race anew. This time he does not form the human race from scratch, as in chapter 2, but he uses Noah and his family, like a baker of sourdough bread using some of the old yeast starter for the new batch. The outcome is not the obliteration of the human race but a new arrangement between God and human beings, who are still made in his image (8:20—9:17).

The flood story may be read as an answer to the question, "Why doesn't God put an end to the world when human beings' inhumanity toward each other descends to intolerable depths?" Surely this question has troubled many people in the course of history as they were driven onto slave ships or herded into gas chambers. To answer the question, the biblical story explores a test case: suppose society became *utterly* corrupt. What would God do? The story suggests that, at least from the human point of view, God would show a certain ambivalence. He would bring judgment, yet he would wish human life to continue. God's rescue of Noah shows that despite human wrongdoing, God is more inclined to save than to judge. Part of the answer, then, to why God allows the world to roll along despite human crimes is that he is constantly looking for ways to make a new start with his wayward human creatures.

God makes clear his policy of patience toward human beings as the story comes to an end (8:21–22; 9:11–17). In 8:21 God shows the universal love that Jesus remarked on: God "makes his sun rise on the evil and on the good, and sends rain on the righteous and on the unrighteous"—a policy of forbearance that Jesus calls us to imitate (Matthew 5:44–45).

Questions for Application

1 What, if anything, can students learn about themselves when they have failed or done badly on a test or in a course?

2 Why are fresh starts so important to us? How can they be opportunities to experience new gifts from God?

3 What are some of the right things to do at the start of the school year to help make it a good year? What are some of the wrong things to do?

4 What can individual students do to make their school a more just place? What might you be able to do as an adult to make the world more just?

Approach to Prayer

Reflect silently for a moment on a social injustice about which you are particularly concerned. Then, along with the group, recite this prayer for social justice composed by Pope Pius XII:

Almighty and eternal God, may your grace
enkindle in all persons a love
of the many unfortunate people
whom poverty and misery reduce
to a condition of life unworthy of human beings.

Arouse in the hearts
of those who call you God
a hunger and thirst for social justice
and for fraternal charity in deeds and in truth.

Grant, O Lord, peace in our days,
peace to souls, peace to our community
and peace among nations.

Saints in the Making

An Ark for Today

In 1964 a Canadian named Jean Vanier invited two men with mental and physical disabilities, Raphael and Philippe, to live with him. With Vanier providing the necessary care, the men kept house together, did a little gardening, cooked their meals, went to church, and prayed the rosary.

Vanier wrote afterward, "The idea of living happily together, of celebrating and laughing a lot, came quickly and spontaneously." Vanier's attitude shifted from simply *doing* things for the men to *listening* to them. "When the idea of the poor educating us came, I don't know exactly," Vanier wrote. "The words of Saint Vincent de Paul, 'The poor are our masters,' were always there, but when they became a reality I'm uncertain."

"During those first months," Vanier recalled, "I was beginning to discover the immense amount of pain hidden in the hearts of Raphael and Philippe. At the same time I was beginning to discover some of the beauty and gentleness of their hearts, their capacity for communion and tenderness. I was beginning to sense how living with them could transform me."

Women in Trosly-Breuil, the French town where the men were living, brought gifts of food. A religious sister volunteered to cook meals. Vanier welcomed a third man with disabilities. A former art student, Jacqueline d'Halluin, began to come regularly to share in the work of the little household.

Vanier asked d'Halluin to write a prayer and help him choose a name for the budding community. The prayer she wrote addressed Our Lady: "Mary, give us hearts that are attentive, humble, and gentle, so that we may welcome with tenderness and compassion all the poor you send us." D'Halluin suggested about a hundred names, drawn from the Bible. As soon as she mentioned the ark, Vanier knew that she had found the right name. "But it was only later on that I realized all the symbolism behind this biblical name," Vanier recalled.

Since 1964 the community of adults with disabilities and those who share their lives has grown and spread to many countries around the world. It is generally identified by the French form of its name: L'Arche (The Ark).

Between
Discussions

We can easily imagine that Noah and his family had a lot to keep them busy when they emerged from the ark—letting the animals go, unloading their belongings, setting up housekeeping in the mud. The narrator passes over such practical matters, however, and describes an action of a different sort. Noah built an altar, slaughtered animals, and burned them on the altar for God (8:20). This was the first act of humankind in the creation renewed after the flood.

You may recall that this is not the first mention of sacrifice in these Genesis stories of beginnings. Earlier, Cain and Abel made offerings to God from flock and field (4:3–4).

Cain and Abel made their offerings in the course of the seasonal pattern of their lives, as crops matured and flocks reproduced and grew. Noah's offering was directed toward marking a unique event: the salvation of his family. Both types of sacrifice served the same purpose: acknowledging that God is the source of life. The regular offerings of vegetables and fruit, sheep and cattle expressed the awareness that the vitality and fertility of plants and animals come from God. Noah's onetime offering on the damp hilltop was his way of acknowledging that he and his family owed their lives to God's action on their behalf in the events of the flood.

These sacrifices connect with an important theme in Genesis—our being created in the image and likeness of God (1:26–27). We will never fully understand what it means to resemble God because we will never fully understand the God we resemble. But two aspects of our resemblance to him are in the foreground of the Genesis narrative.

First, in the ancient Near East, kings were considered images of God. For humans to be made in the image of God, then, means that we are placed here as royalty. We are commissioned to rule the earth on God's behalf. The earth will fulfill God's purposes as we rule it under his direction.

Second, our being made in the image of God means that there is a match, a fit, between God and us that makes us capable of having a personal relationship with him. This makes us different from all the other creatures of the earth. We are the only creatures that can recognize that the universe belongs to God and thank and praise him for his blessings.

The first aspect of our being made in God's image has us acting on behalf of God *toward creation,* caring for the earth according to his purposes. The second aspect has us acting on behalf of creation *toward God,* offering him thanks on behalf of the rest of creation.

The Genesis stories show that the first human beings carried out their roles imperfectly, as have all of us since then. God continues to want the human race to play its assigned role, so he sent his Son to become one of us to play our part perfectly. As a human being like us, Jesus led a life of perfect love for other people, of perfect use of this world for God's purposes. Then he died as an offering of obedience to God, acknowledging that God is the giver of life, trusting that God would raise him up again. Thus Jesus fulfilled God's desire to have a perfect human representative *to his creation* and a perfect human offering of praise and thanksgiving *to God.* Jesus fulfilled both the earthward and the Godward roles for which God created us.

Now, as we are united with Jesus, God restores our ability to rule the earth according to his purposes and to live our lives in praise and thanks to him. It was in Jesus' death on the cross that he showed both God's love to the world and his own love for the Father. Jesus' death was a great act of sacrifice. In the Eucharist, we share in Jesus' sacrifice. He draws us into his perfect offering of himself to his Father; united with Jesus, we offer God thanks and praise for all he has made. At the same time, he nourishes us with his body and blood, enabling us to go forth and communicate God's peace and love to the world. In the Eucharist, the sacrifice that surpasses all the sacrifices of Genesis, God restores our ability to live out the earthward and Godward roles for which he has created us.

The End of the Beginning

Warm-Up Questions

1 Are there any students at your school who have difficulty speaking English? What do you think it would be like to go to school in a country whose language you do not speak?

2 What other things besides language get in the way of people communicating with each other?

Opening the Bible

What's Happened

The accounts of Adam and Eve and Cain and Abel deal with paradoxical facts of life. We humans desire to live forever, yet we die. Through work we fulfill God's purposes, yet work is hard and wearying. Childbirth—in which we are privileged to be cocreators with God—is accompanied by pain. Technology—by which we fulfill our assignment to rule the world—often has negative consequences. Why? The Genesis accounts point to a single answer. It was not the Creator who introduced these regrettable contradictions into the human condition. Somehow—the Genesis accounts declare it without explaining it—we humans have undermined our own happiness by violating our God-given purposes and limitations.

After tracing some genealogies (chapter 10) the narrator now examines one further question about the human condition. Why do human beings, who have such marvelous God-given intelligence and belong basically to one family, often fail to understand each other? By this point in our reading, the answer should come as no surprise.

THE READING

Genesis 11:1—12:5

The Clash of Wills with God Continues

^{11:1} Now the whole earth had one language and the same words. ² And as they migrated from the east, they came upon a plain in the land of Shinar and settled there. ³ And they said to one another, "Come, let us make bricks, and burn them thoroughly." And they had brick for stone, and bitumen for mortar. ⁴ Then they said, "Come, let us build ourselves a city, and a tower with its top in the heavens, and let us make a name for ourselves; otherwise we shall be scattered abroad upon the face of the whole earth." ⁵ The LORD came down to see the city and the tower, which mortals had built. ⁶ And the LORD said, "Look, they are one people, and they have all one language; and this is only the beginning of what they

will do; nothing that they propose to do will now be impossible for them. ⁷ Come, let us go down, and confuse their language there, so that they will not understand one another's speech." ⁸ So the LORD scattered them abroad from there over the face of all the earth, and they left off building the city. ⁹ Therefore it was called Babel, because there the LORD confused the language of all the earth; and from there the LORD scattered them abroad over the face of all the earth. . . .

Abraham and Sarah Respond to God

²⁷ Now these are the descendants of Terah. Terah was the father of Abram, Nahor, and Haran; and Haran was the father of Lot. ²⁸ Haran died before his father Terah in the land of his birth, in Ur of the Chaldeans. ²⁹ Abram and Nahor took wives; the name of Abram's wife was Sarai, and the name of Nahor's wife was Milcah. She was the daughter of Haran the father of Milcah and Iscah. ³⁰ Now Sarai was barren; she had no child.

³¹ Terah took his son Abram and his grandson Lot son of Haran, and his daughter-in-law Sarai, his son Abram's wife, and they went out together from Ur of the Chaldeans to go into the land of Canaan; but when they came to Haran, they settled there. ³² The days of Terah were two hundred five years; and Terah died in Haran.

¹²:¹ Now the LORD said to Abram, "Go from your country and your kindred and your father's house to the land that I will show you. ² I will make of you a great nation, and I will bless you, and make your name great, so that you will be a blessing. ³ I will bless those who bless you, and the one who curses you I will curse; and in you all the families of the earth shall be blessed."

⁴ So Abram went, as the LORD had told him; and Lot went with him. Abram was seventy-five years old when he departed from Haran. ⁵ Abram took his wife Sarai and his brother's son Lot, and all the possessions that they had gathered, and the persons whom they had acquired in Haran; and they set forth to go to the land of Canaan.

Questions for a Closer Look

1 Compare what the people want to avoid (11:4) with God's command to them (1:28; 9:1).

2 Compare Abraham's response to God in 12:1–5 with that of the people in 11:2–4.

3 How does God's problem with the people at Shinar compare to the problem he faced with Adam and Eve (3:4,22)? In what ways are the Eden and Babel stories similar?

A Guide to the Reading

God directed the first human beings to fill the earth (1:28; 9:1). But this does not suit the people at Shinar, who prefer to stay together and build a monument to their own greatness (11:4).

Just like Adam and Eve, the people in Shinar choose independence rather than obedience and trust in God. They want to exercise godlike control over their lives. The tower of Babel confirms what God had observed after the flood: "The inclination of the human heart is evil from youth" (8:21).

The tower of Babel story reflects the architecture and religion of Mesopotamia (present-day Iraq). The setting might have sounded as exotic to the story's original readers as it does to us. Notice that the narrator finds it necessary to explain why the people planned to use bricks and asphalt: "they had brick for stone, and bitumen for mortar" (11:3). Israelite readers were not acquainted with brick construction. In Israel there was plenty of stone and little water, so people did not generally build with bricks. Bricks were, however, the main building material in Mesopotamia, which had less stone but plenty of mud. The Israelites, who lived in a hilly land, were probably also unfamiliar with the idea of building impressive towers for religious purposes. In Mesopotamia, however, where the land was relatively flat, people constructed artificial mountains—towers—to serve as high places where humans might make contact with the gods.

The people at Shinar try to be godlike, but their attempt is a pathetic failure. As tall as their tower seems to them, its height is insignificant to God, who has to go "down" to examine it (11:5). As always, the refusal to obey God ends in disaster (11:7–9). The story makes the point that if we reject the God who brings order out of chaos, our relationships with one another will become chaotic.

Various details reinforce this message. For example, the Hebrew word for bricks (11:3) is echoed in the word for confuse (11:7). This subtly suggests that grasping for godlike status ensures its doom. Evil is a boomerang.

The account of the people who built the tower of Babel is different from the earlier stories because it ends without consolation. God made clothes for the first couple; he put a mark of protection on the first murderer; he established a covenant with the survivors of the flood. But the Babel story breaks off without any softening of the judgment. We are left to wonder whether God has any further plans for his wayward human creatures. Has a basically hopeless dynamic now been established for human history? Will God's masterpieces—human beings—simply continue to grieve him by overstepping their creaturely limits and playing god over their own lives? These marvelous creatures, who are still in God's image and still cocreators and co-workers with him, now live under the shadow of pain, toil, disharmony, and death. Does God plan to straighten out this sad situation?

With the appearance of Terah (11:27), we have arrived at a new era. The narrative leaves behind parable-like stories of origins and emerges onto the stage of history. Events now occur in historical places, such as Ur and Haran (in present-day Iraq and Turkey, 11:31). The focus narrows from the ancestors of the entire human race to one particular family—the family of Terah's son Abram, ancestor of the people Israel. With the first 11 chapters fresh in our minds, we may well suspect that God's dealings with this one family will have implications for the whole world.

Abraham believes God's promises and responds to God's summons (12:1–4; it is customary to refer to Abram and Sarai by the adjusted names God later gives them: Abraham and Sarah, 17:5,15). With his wife, Abraham rejects the distrust and disobedience toward God that have caused problems for people. Thus he sets the standard for human responses to the plan that God is going to unfold. For God does indeed have a plan to straighten out the mess that human sin has caused—a plan that will culminate in Jesus of Nazareth's perfect trust in and obedience to God.

Questions for Application

1 What causes young people to sometimes have difficulty communicating with their parents? How does each party help create a barrier to honest communication? What can they do to overcome the barrier?

2 The biblical text suggests that the people at Shinar did not understand each other because they did not listen to one another. How much of the misunderstandings between people stem from not listening? What can they do to increase the degree in which they truly hear what other people are saying?

3 How might following God's commandments help in your relationships with other people?

4 God called Abraham to leave behind what was familiar and enter into a totally unfamiliar area. You will probably have to enter unfamiliar areas at different times in your life. How can you best prepare yourself to meet those challenges?

Approach to Prayer

The gift of the Holy Spirit, given to Jesus' followers after his return to the Father, can reverse the confusion and division of Babel. Pray for the Spirit to work in your own relationships.

Listen as a member of the group reads the account of Pentecost, which describes the Spirit beginning to undo the language barrier thrown up as a consequence of human pride at Babel (Acts 2:1–11).

Then, if you wish, mention relationships in which there is bitterness or misunderstanding. After each one, pray with the group, "Come, Holy Spirit, bring healing, hearing, and understanding."

End by praying the Our Father together.

Saints in the Making

Young Missionary

Adults are not the only ones who go to faraway places to spread the good news of God's love. Children and young people also leave home, often accompanying their parents on missionary assignments.

Joseph Miya is one such young missionary, living with his parents and his four siblings in Tanzania. His parents are lay missionaries working with the Maryknoll Order of priests, brothers, and sisters. While his parents are busy doing their missionary work, Joseph is making new friends. "You get to meet new people and make lots of friends. You end up liking your friends more than you would think you would. I like playing soccer with the boys in my neighborhood. In the dry season we play soccer in the rice paddy down the street from our house. In the rainy season we play in a field up the road."

There is another side to Joseph's life far from home, for he gets to join in the missionary work. "The thing I like most about being a missionary kid is that you get to join in all the activities your mission does; like celebrating holidays together, scavenger hunts, and huge parties for birthdays." He even does some good work among his friends. "I once told my friends that candy is bad for your health, that you should eat peanuts instead. Ever since then, they've been eating peanuts."

Joseph sees some personal benefits coming out of his missionary stay in Tanzania. "Being a missionary kid means that you get a lifetime of education which helps you go through life easier. For example, how to help each other through hard times, like when you are moving. Also, having friends from different countries is educational."

Since the days of Saint Paul, Christians have been leaving home to be Christ to people in other countries. Some of them have done serious and heavy work, such as running medical clinics, managing building projects, and teaching. But sometimes the best missionary work consists in simply being a friend and allowing God's love to shine through your friendship. Young Joseph Miya is that kind of missionary.

After Words

I t would be hard to exaggerate the importance of Abraham. The term *pivotal figure* might have been created to describe him.

The period of the beginning of the human race comes to an end when Abraham appears in Genesis 12. With the story of Abraham and Sarah, God's action in historical times gets under way. Unlike Adam, Eve, Cain, Abel, and Noah, Abraham is not an ancestor of the human race. He is simply one of the thousands of sheep and cattle breeders who lived in eastern Syria roughly 4,000 years ago. Abraham and Sarah are ordinary people, called by God to play a part in his grand plan for the human race. Since Abraham, God has been active in the world, running through the history of Israel, culminating in the saving acts of Jesus of Nazareth, and continuing through the life of the Church.

Abraham was the ancestor of the Israelites. It was one of his grandsons, Jacob, also called Israel, who gave his name to the people. Members of Israel referred to themselves as descendants of Abraham—an expression of identity heard in the Gospels (John 8:33).

In the history of Israel, however, another figure looms larger: Moses. He leads the people of Israel through the events that formed them as a people: the escape from Egypt and the covenant with God at Sinai. Moses is considered the author of the first five books of the Bible, which record the basic instruction for Israel's life with God. Since the people's relationship with God centers on a reverent application of this instruction to their lives, Moses occupies a central position for the people of Israel.

For Christians, Jesus displaced Moses from this central role. Jesus respected the Mosaic law but taught that it did not perfectly reflect God's intentions for human life (Matthew 5:17–48). Jesus offered himself in fulfillment of the law—the model of complete trust in and obedience to God and of perfect love for human beings. Jesus died and rose and gave us his Spirit so that we might have a relationship with God even deeper than that shaped by the Mosaic instruction (Hebrews 10:12–17).

Saint Paul tells us that Jesus brought to completion the period of God's plan that began with Moses. God's activity reached its climax in Jesus, Paul says, and therefore God's people should live not in faithfulness to the Mosaic law but in imitation of Abraham's example, which will always remain valid (Galatians 3). Jesus' followers should look back past Moses to Abraham, with whom God's activity had begun.

Abraham and Sarah listened to God, they believed what God promised them, and they did what God told them to do. These are the reasons the New Testament writers point to Abraham as our model and spiritual ancestor (Galatians 3:6; James 2:21–24).

Abraham and Sarah were challenged to believe the virtually impossible. How could they, who had had no children during the long years of their marriage, have offspring from whom a great people would arise? They could only act on this promise by having complete trust in God as the Lord and giver of life (see Hebrews 11:8–12,17–19). Thus Abraham and Sarah show us what our response to God should be like.

There will be times in our lives when, in order to follow Jesus, we will have to leave behind beloved people and things and go where God leads us. We will have to face the questions of whether we can trust God's ability to create new life, whether God has a plan for our lives, and whether God will be faithful. Abraham and Sarah faced and answered these same questions. We can take this couple as our model.

Through Abraham's and Sarah's trust and obedience, God set in motion a plan for all humankind. Who knows what part of that plan God might accomplish through our willingness to hear an unexpected call from him, through our obedience and trust.

A Book for Today

The Bible has been described as the user's manual for the universe. That statement is half right. The Bible is not a handbook containing how-to answers to all our questions. But it is the Creator's basic written message to us concerning his purposes for our lives and his relationship with us.

The opening chapters of Genesis were written two and a half millennia ago and do not deal directly with specific modern issues. Nevertheless, they are quite relevant to issues we face today. The 11 opening chapters convey a great deal about God's intentions and his view of us—an invaluable background for our thinking. Here are observations on three areas where Genesis touches on modern concerns.

The environment ~ We have become very aware in recent decades of the damage to the environment caused by humans. Some people have accused the Bible of contributing to the problem. Critics especially target Genesis 1. They claim that the Bible has exposed nature to human exploitation by insisting that there is only one God above the entire universe. Take away the gods of rain, soil, and fertility, and nature no longer seems sacred, only useful. Critics also charge that the command to humanity to "subdue" and "have dominion over" the earth (1:28) has enabled us to justify our disregard for the damage we inflict on the environment.

It may well be true that people have sometimes appealed to the Bible to defend exploitation of the environment. If so, however, the problem lies not in the Bible itself but in false interpretations of the Bible.

Replacing the nature gods with faith in the one God does not expose the earth to abuse, for the earth belongs to God. God puts the man in the garden to "keep," or protect, it (2:15), not to destroy it. The man is a caretaker, responsible to the owner for maintaining the property in good condition.

God's command to us to rule the earth is not a license to mistreat the natural world. There is not to be a ruthless dominance but rather a domination modeled on God's domination of the universe. The creation accounts show God ordering the universe and approving its purposefulness. We, as his representatives, are responsible for understanding and maintaining God's order and achieving his purposes for creation.

When Genesis shows God establishing humans as kings over the earth, the intention was not to propose unrestrained power and authority. We are to be the kind of kings that the Israelite kings were supposed to be, shepherding the people, not oppressing them. Humanity is supposed to care for the earth, not rape it.

If we read Genesis 1 carefully, then, we will respect and not misuse the environment. However, some of our efforts at fostering harmony between humans and the natural world run counter to the viewpoint of Genesis. It is good to emphasize our dependence on the environment and to protect other living things from abuse, but some environmentalists seem to propose a kind of equality between humans and other life-forms. They speak of humans as simply one of earth's many species, with no more or less right to live than any of the others. The Genesis accounts, however, draw a sharp, distinguishing line between the human race and all other species.

The creation account in Genesis 1 shows that God assigns a unique status to the human race. Humans alone are created in the image and likeness of God, which gives us a unique relationship with God and an assignment to rule the earth (1:27–28). The account in Genesis 2 reinforces the distinction between humanity and other species. God brings the animals before the man to be named, thus showing the man's authority over them. Among the animals, "there was not found a helper as his partner" (2:20) because there is a basic difference between a human being and an animal.

Sex ~ Genesis says nothing directly about the various sexual issues we face in the modern world. But, again, it provides invaluable background for our thinking.

Consider, for example, the widespread acceptance of sex outside marriage, in light of these elements of the Genesis account:

➤ According to Genesis 2, the purpose of human sexuality lies in man and woman becoming so united as to be "one flesh" (2:24).

➤ The account suggests that the bond between the man and the woman provides the opportunity for them to know themselves as they otherwise could not. The text suggests that in coming to know the woman the man comes to know himself.

➤ The narrator says that the man knows his wife (4:1). This term for sexual intercourse is not a way of speaking about sex indirectly—it is a term of great significance. The biblical writers never speak of animals as *knowing* their sexual partners. *Knowing* indicates the personal, more-than-biological dimension of human sexuality. The term testifies to the profoundly relational quality of human sex.

It is clear that God intends for the human sexual relationships to have some depth. Doesn't the uncommitted, casual, or recreational use of sex seem to fall short of what God intended?

Another subject to which Genesis is relevant is the Catholic teaching about the link between sexual intercourse and reproduction. The Church teaches that, in God's purposes, intercourse and reproduction belong together. The person-uniting and person-creating aspects of human sex cannot be separated. Artificial contraception represents one attempt to deliberately separate these two aspects of sex; artificial insemination represents another. The Church teaches us that neither attempt is moral.

Many Catholics find it hard to accept this teaching. It seems implausible to them that there could be *any* good reason to refrain from using available technologies to control what could be controlled in this area of life. Living in a technological culture, many Catholics are used to maximizing their control over every aspect of life. It seems normal to them to use technology whenever it can help us achieve their purposes. With this mind-set, they cannot be convinced that we should not use technology to determine such an important area of our lives as sex and reproduction.

Two aspects of the Genesis accounts raise questions about this almost automatic tendency to take technological control of our sexuality. First is the profound interest that God takes in human sexuality. Sex is, indeed, the first topic on which God speaks to human beings: "God blessed them, and God said to them, 'Be fruitful and multiply, and fill the earth'" (1:28). The blessing that God gives the first couple is a sharing in his own creative power. God's blessing is the capacity he gives us to fulfill his command to be fruitful, the fertility that he places within us (compare 1:22). In the process of having children, we are cocreators with God, as Eve recognized when she greeted Cain's birth with words that may be translated, "I have created a man with the Lord" (4:1).

The second consideration is our desire to take control of our lives, as portrayed in Genesis 3. When the man and the woman are told not to eat from the tree of the knowledge of good and evil, the issue is whether they will acknowledge a creaturely limit to their freedom. They cannot fully understand this limit and will only be able to keep it in a spirit of obedience to and trust in God.

These considerations can help us as we reflect on the Church's teaching against artificially separating the person-uniting and person-creating dimensions of sex. Neither consideration speaks directly to the issues involved, but they can help us to examine the teaching in a different frame of mind from that of our technological culture. Genesis reminds us that in our sexuality we touch on something especially important to God. Our creator is profoundly present with us in this dimension of our lives. Should we not, then, be especially serious in searching out God's purposes for our sexuality? The drama in the garden invites us to recognize our inclination to violate creaturely limits and play god over our lives. Might this inclination be at work in our modern attitudes toward sex and reproduction?

Human life ~ Abortion and capital punishment are currently divisive issues in our society. In Genesis we find much that is significant for both issues.

Actually, the fundamental question about abortion is not religious but biological: is the fetus a human being? The science of embryology has made it clear that the fetus is indeed a human being. Once we accept the scientific finding that the fetus is a separate human life, Genesis helps us understand how we should treat this life.

Genesis tells us that God created the human race in his image and likeness. In the biblical tradition it has always been recognized that each individual shares in this divine likeness. Reflecting on this tradition, ancient Jewish sages wrote that to save a single life is to save the whole world.

God's response to Abel's murder makes clear how seriously God regards the destruction of a single human life (4:10–11). And God's protection of Cain (4:13–15) shows how highly God continues to value the life even of one who has taken life. This point leads us to consider how the Genesis accounts might speak to the issue of capital punishment.

Although God protects Cain from vengeance, farther on in the narrative (in the story of Noah), God gives instructions for the execution of murderers (9:5–6). This action might seem to contradict God's approach toward Cain, but the underlying principle in both passages is the same: human life is inviolable because it belongs to God. The imposition of capital punishment in chapter 9 has become necessary to defend life because human beings have become so violent (6:11).

Capital punishment was practiced throughout the ancient Near East, as it has been in many societies throughout history. Capital punishment, slavery, warfare that placed civilian populations under the ban—these and other inhumane practices marred the early stages of the Israelite tradition. They were reflections of the cultural environment from which the community was coming, not the purposes of God toward which it was journeying. The revelation of God's mercy and love worked gradually within the community of faith as a leavening element—as it continues to do today.

Regarding capital punishment, the element from Genesis that has enduring validity is the principle that humans are created in God's image, not the instruction to impose capital punishment. God's treatment of Cain demonstrates his preference for protecting the life even of someone who has killed. Today it is possible to protect human life without imposing capital punishment for murder. The call in contemporary Catholic teaching to end capital punishment in virtually all situations is in keeping with the biblical tradition, which emphasizes the value of each human life.

Listening When God Speaks

As you have worked your way through this book, you have been listening to God's word. But this is not the first time that God has spoken to you, and indeed God has been speaking to you throughout your young life. Let's look at some of the ways in which God speaks to you, and let's look at some of the ways in which you can improve your listening skills

The most obvious way in which you receive messages from God is through the Scripture, which is the Word of God. The people of Israel and the early Christians recorded their experiences of God's saving acts in history, and our religious tradition accepts their writings as God's Word to us. We believe that when we read Scripture, or hear it read, God is communicating his Word to us. It would be a good thing for you to develop the habit of reading the Bible on a regular basis, and you should make every effort to benefit from the weekly reading of Scripture at Mass.

An excellent way in which to listen to God speaking to us in Scripture is to pray the Scripture. Begin by adopting a proper prayer *posture* through the selection of an appropriate time and place for prayer. Once in the proper posture, become aware of God's *presence* in your life and in the time and place you have chosen for your prayer. Then *pray* for guidance from the Holy Spirit, asking help to understand the passage you will be reading and reflecting on. You are now ready to read your selected *passage,* but you must read slowly and deliberately, with the intention of hearing God's voice in the passage. After you have read and reread the passage, *pause* for reflection on the passage. Allow time for God to speak to you through the words of the text.

The Bible is the Word of God, but it is not the only Word of God. Jesus Christ is also the Word of God, the Word made flesh. The Gospel of John begins with that message: "In the beginning was the Word, and the Word was with God, and the Word was

God. . . . And the Word became flesh and made his dwelling among us." We want, then, to listen to God speaking to us in Jesus Christ and one good way to do that is by participating fully in Mass. Gathering together with the other worshipers, we enter into communion with them and with the presiding priest. The words and actions of the celebration put our spirits at rest, so that by the time we enter into communion with Christ in the Eucharist, we are in a position to hear God's message of love, peace, and salvation. We should not make the mistake of thinking that Jesus speaks to us only at the moment of receiving the Eucharist. His voice can be heard—if only we listen—through the community, through the priest, through the entire Eucharistic celebration, and finally, bringing it all together, in the eating and drinking of the Body and Blood of Christ.

Because the Church is the Body of Christ, we can also speak of the Church as the Word of God. God speaks to us through the community of believers, and in a special way through the leadership of that community. One way to listen to the voice of God in the Church is by paying attention to the voices of the believers nearest us: our parents and teachers, our parish priest, and the people we worship with on Sunday. Another way is to stay in touch with what the leadership of our Church is teaching. The bishops of our Church, especially the bishop of Rome, the Holy Father, and our own local bishop, the leader of the Church where we are active, speak to us in words that have the authority of the Word of God, and as Catholics we hear in them the voice of God.

Finally, God speaks to us in our own life experiences. The Second Vatican Council recovered the biblical image of "reading the signs of the times," that is, hearing the voice of God in the events of history. On the personal level, we can hear God speaking to us in such things as our encounters with others, our decisions, our successes and failures, and the challenges arising from the difficulties of life. To hear God's voice in our life experiences, we need to pay attention to those experiences, reflect on them, and learn from them.

There is a wonderful story in the Old Testament about a young boy named Samuel. (You can read it in 1 Samuel 3.) Samuel was assisting an old priest named Eli, who was waiting in the temple for God to speak to him. One night while he was sleeping, Samuel heard someone call him. He assumed it was Eli, so he went and woke Eli up to find out what he wanted. Eli responded that he had not called, and he sent the boy back to bed. After a while Samuel heard his name called again, but once more Eli told the boy that it was not him. When it happened a third time, Eli knew that it was God calling to Samuel and he said to the boy, "Go to sleep, and if you are called, reply, 'Speak, LORD, for your servant is listening.'"

The first thing to notice about this story is that everybody expected God to speak to the old priest, but God spoke to the young boy instead. It is important that you be receptive in your youth to the voice of God and not think that God will only speak to you "later." God is speaking to you now—in the Scriptures, in Jesus Christ, in the Church, and in your life experiences.

The other point of the story is that, in order to hear God speaking to us, we must be listening. Samuel would never have received God's message if he had not listened, and the same thing applies to us. Ours is a busy life, with plenty of noise. We need to learn how to cut through all the noise and listen to God speaking to us.

Resources

Bibles

The following editions of the Bible contain the full set of biblical books recognized by the Catholic Church, along with a great deal of useful explanatory material:

➤ The Catholic Youth Bible (Saint Mary's Press), which can be ordered with either the New American Bible or the New Revised Standard Version

➤ Student Bible for Catholics (Thomas Nelson Publishers), which uses the text of the New American Bible

➤ The Catholic Study Bible (Oxford University Press), which uses the text of the New American Bible

➤ The Catholic Bible: Personal Study Edition (Oxford University Press), which also uses the text of the New American Bible

Additional Sources

➤ Philipps, James. "Genesis: First Book of Our Faith," *Youth Update,* Cincinnati, OH: St. Anthony Messenger Press, March 1999.

➤ Viviano, Pauline A. *Genesis.* Collegeville, MN: The Liturgical Press, 1983.